Chris G. Panos . . . stood at the gate and watched as the Communist guard thumbed through the Bible.

"You got any more books?" the guard asked.

"Yes, I do," Panos replied.

The guard studied the Bible a moment longer in the dim light and handed it back to Panos.

"Move on," he said.

And Panos moved on, into a country that does not take too well to people who bring in Bibles.

"The Lord just says, 'Go ye into these countries' . . . He doesn't say anything about coming back."

—*Tommy West,* in THE HOUSTON POST

"Call it luck, call it coincidence, but Panos calls the manner in which he gets his Bibles past Communist guards and custom officials a miracle and 'God's will.' "

—*Charlotta Becker,*
in THE COLUMBUS DISPATCH

"He gives the Lord credit for everything. . . . 'The Lord provides, the Lord led me, the Lord opened the way' is his invariable response."

—*Jean Culbertson,*
in THE MISSISSIPPI CLARION-LEDGER

Faith under
FIRE

by Chris Panos

Whitaker House
co-published with, Auxosia Book

Copyright © 1974
Printed in United States of America
ISBN number 0-88368-038-6

Co-published by:

WHITAKER HOUSE   **AUXOSIA BOOKS**
504 Laurel Drive   Suite 1509, 600 Jefferson Bldg.
Monroeville   Cullen Center
Pennsylvania 15146   Houston, Texas 77002

1st printing 10,000
2nd printing 15,000

Unless otherwise indicated, all Scripture quotations in this volume
are from the King James Version of the Bible.

Scripture quotations identified as AMPLIFIED are from The
Amplified New Testament © 1958 The Lockman Foundation.
Used by permission.

Some of the names of people and places in this book
have been changed to protect the individuals involved.
The events are absolutely as described.

This Book Is
Dedicated
To The Men of God
Who Influenced My Ministry
In Person and
Through Their Writings

Charles Price	Smith Wigglesworth
E. W. Kenyon	F. F. Bosworth
Gordon Lindsay	Thomas Wyatt
George Mueller	Charles Finney

John Lake

Billy Graham	Morris Cerullo
Oral Roberts	T. L. Osborn
Brother Andrew	John Osteen
Harald Bredesen	Pat Robertson

and

Our Deepest Appreciation to
Mary W. Stephens
and
Linda F. Veselka

CONTENTS

FOREWORD
By Harald Bredesen

Have you ever exclaimed as you read great exploits of faith, "Oh, if I could have faith like that!" Then this book is for you. This book is written for the person who knows that faith is the golden key which unlocks every treasure in the storehouse of God and every weapon in His arsenal—and who, having tried to wield that key, has failed. It will tell him how to try again, this time successfully, as it tells how to lay hold of that very faith which has carried Chris Panos over so many hurdles and through so many dangers to such remarkable experiences.

CHAPTER 1

MILLIONS AND MIRACLES

The Bible says, "Knock and it shall be opened unto you." The source of supply for the Christian has always been heaven. Whatever we can loose there will be supplied to us here. This has always been the case: there has never been an instance where the supplies of heaven were too depleted to meet the needs of any and all believers.

If you are a child of God today, you hold in your hand a master key that will open every door. Nothing can keep you in, and nothing can keep you out. I know that this is true for two very good reasons: first, the Bible says so. And second, I have found it to be true throughout my life as a child of God.

I was not always a child of God. Although I had had an encounter with Christ as a child, as a young man I forgot all that. Lonely, perplexed, and confused, I continued to grow deeper into a life of sin. Having grown up in the restaurant business, I was determined to become a millionaire early in life. So I married my sweet wife, Earnestine, and went to work at earning money. Before I settled on building and real estate, I had tried my hand at the restaurant business, boots and shoes and even the shoeshine business.

As I made a success of real estate, I began to accumulate stock, real estate, and luxurious material possessions. And I also began to drink, to smoke, to gamble, and to sin in a social way. As the president of many corporations, I felt self-sufficient. I had decided that I didn't need God—or anybody else.

One night my wife had a dream that the Lord Jesus Christ was coming back. She awoke screaming, "Lord Jesus, don't come back yet, I am not ready. I am not under Your grace! I am not baptized!"

When she told me her dream, I thought it was a nightmare.

But, far from being a nightmare, Earnestine's dream was from the Lord; and no matter what I said about it (and I said plenty!) it was sufficient to cause my wife to receive Jesus Christ as her Lord and Savior.

How my wife changed! She began to read the Bible and pray—and she began to pray for me. Then she began to attend prayer meetings. And *then* she started to hold prayer meetings in our own house.

At the time, I thought my wife was crazy. Now, of course I know she wasn't crazy. *I* was crazy, because I wouldn't listen. It wasn't only my wife I was ignoring; I was ignoring the Lord Himself. God had worked miracles for me already, and I had forgotten them all—I had completely forgotten, totally pushed out of my mind, the fact that He had already saved my life at least once, and that as a child I had even seen the Lord.

In the sight of God, I am sure that every birth is a miracle. But my birth really *was* a miracle. I was born to a Greek Orthodox family in Galveston, Texas, and the doctors had given me up for dead. But the Lord Jesus Christ appeared to my mother in a vision as she lay in the hospital.

The Lord spoke and said to her, "Fear not, the child will not die, but the child will live. Do not name him Patrick after your father but name him Christos." So my mother named me Christos, which is Greek for Christ, and that is how I came to be named after the Lord.

Then my mother called my father and told him the good news about how the Lord had appeared to her in a vision. Both of them were filled with joy and excitement. They knew that if I were to live, it would take a miracle of God. A miracle is what they got! The doctor decided to take one last try to save my life: he put a small rubber hose into my mouth and drew out all the mucus that had clogged my lungs.

As my father tells it, I was lying on the shelf like a brick—"But suddenly Christos began to kick, and he is still kicking today."

My boyhood days were quick and furious. I escaped death's door many times. From an early age, I was trained in the restaurant business to work hard and make money. My heart began to grow hard as steel.

One day when I was around nine, I had gone down

to the dime store and was looking at all the pretty toys. I walked up to a counter that had metal soldiers and fortresses on it—and, since I wanted them and didn't have the money to pay for them—I took the ones I wanted, put them in a sack, and walked out of the store knowing that no one had seen me.

On my way back to my father's restaurant, I passed by the city park in Fort Worth, Texas. Suddenly I had a strong urge to turn to the right. As I turned, I saw a beautiful tall man, dressed in white, looking at me. His arms stretched out towards me, bidding me to come to Him.

In the twinkling of an eye, I felt guilty and frightened. I didn't know what to do. I was frozen stiff. Then—without knowing whether I ran or flew—suddenly there I was across the street, face to face with Him. I saw tears running down His precious cheeks.

Boy, was I scared! I had never seen any other man like this before. I took off and ran down the street until I got to my parents' restaurant. I ran inside screaming, "I saw the Lord Jesus!" I burst into tears and cried, "He saw me take the soldiers—He saw me! Mamma, help me! Will He forgive me?"

My mother asked me when and where I had seen the Lord. By this time, as you can imagine, I had captured the attention of all the customers in the restaurant! I told them the whole story. Then my mother and father took me with them and immediately went to the park. When we arrived at the park, the beautiful Man was gone.

Many years passed and I forgot everything: the miracle birth, the encounter with Christ. My wife received the Lord and began to pray for me. For some reason—

maybe it was pride, maybe ambition, I really don't know what it was—I had decided that receiving the Lord was not for me. So for two years my wife prayed, along with many others, asking God to "Save his soul or take him."

God almost took me.

One night as I was driving home, I skidded off the highway into a ditch. I uprooted a tree, broke my jaw in four places and my nose in one, and was near death from internal injuries.

If there is anything I thank God for, it is that He visited me that night. I saw a vision of Calvary, and I realized I was going to hell. The Bible says, "Whosoever shall call upon the name of the Lord shall be saved." I knew the name of the Lord all right. I could forget my miracle birth, and I could forget having seen Jesus as a little boy, but I could not forget the name of the Lord. He had seen to that when He told my mother to name me Christos. I knew His name as well as I knew my own.

But even though I had called on His name, I had very little faith that God would hear me. I was lonely and in despair, and I felt that God was far removed from me. As they rushed me to the hospital, I had no idea how soon I was to meet Him.

As I lay in the hospital, a light suddenly filled the room. There was a supernatural peace filling the whole room. I felt as if I was being elevated into the air. Then

I saw that beautiful Man, with that wonderful love and joy in His eyes.

He stretched out His arm and placed His hand on my hand and said in Greek (the language I understood best), "Chris Panos, I have called you to preach My Bible unto all the world." By that time, I had become so sin-hardened that if He had called me to preach the "Gospel," I wouldn't have known what He meant. Fortunately our Lord never complicates Himself with us, but is always ready to meet us at our own level. So He called me—in Greek—to preach the *Bible*, and I understood Him perfectly.

Needless to say, my whole life changed after that. Like my wife, I began to pray and read the Bible. One night as I was praying, God's presence came down and I began to weep and weep. I had just been reading a magazine in which T.L. Osborn told how he felt he had failed as a missionary to India.

I cried out and said, "Lord, I won't fail You! Use me."

The Lord told me, "You will receive a letter inviting you to come to India to preach. Fear not, only believe: sell all and go, for I am with you."

I literally left all my material possessions behind me: a yearly contract with a $26,000 guarantee, investments, a beautiful house and cars, a rosy future in real estate; everything. Since then I have lived by faith, relying on God to supply my food, my shelter, my own spending money and the money for my crusade campaigns—and He has supplied my every need abundantly!

Since then, I have traveled into forty nations with the Good News, preaching to ones and twos at the Wailing

16

Wall and to crowds of thousands in various large campaigns.

I have smuggled Bibles into all the Red satellite countries of Russia—and into Russia itself.

I have brought the Good News—both spoken and written—into Red China.

And in everything I do, I rely only on God, my Everlasting Source.

If you are a child of God today, you can rely on the same Source I do.

Don't say to yourself, "Well, of course it works for Chris Panos. He had a miracle birth. He saw the Lord." God is no respecter of persons. What He promises to one in His Word, He promises to all. The Bible says, "Ask and it shall be given, seek, and ye shall find, knock and it shall be opened unto you." Dare to knock on every door that seems to be shut, do it in faith in a living Christ, and you will see it swing open for you, just as I have seen it swing open for me.

CHAPTER 2

FAITH THAT WINS

Not long ago, a very good friend of mine asked me, "How can I have peace of mind? What is wrong when I take the stand of faith and nothing happens?"

Everyone who undertakes the walk of faith has such experiences at first. There are times when there is either no answer, or only a partial one. When that happens, what went wrong? I'll tell you: usually, it's because you have been thinking wrong! The Bible tells us: "Whosoever shall say . . . and *shall not doubt* in his heart . . . he shall have whatsoever he saith" (Mark 11:23; italics added).

Miracle Faith Thoughts
Bring Victory in Russia

I remember one time when I was going into Russia, and as I was going through customs I was carrying Bibles in every specially-constructed pocket, as well as in one of my suitcases. I had to smuggle them in, because it's illegal to bring God's Word into Russia.

Well, there I was, going through customs loaded with Bibles. The Russians train their customs agents to detect the slightest irregularities in a traveller's appearance. They watch his facial expression; they watch how he answers his questions. I was defenseless. I knew without a doubt that I was powerless to defend myself except through the power of Christ.

The customs agent took my passport and read it out loud in perfect English, "Chris Panos, Houston, Texas." Then he asked, "Which of these bags is yours?"

I had a little brown suitcase, and I showed it to him. He told me to open it. I opened it. Then he looked at me and said, "What do you have in that other brown bag?" There seemed to be several moments of silence. Suddenly he grabbed the bag, unzipped it, and took out a Bible. In a flash, the Spirit of the Living God moved on my spirit and said, " 'Blind' him in Jesus' name!"

Without hesitation, I "blinded" him in the name of Jesus.

I remembered how the Apostle Paul said to Elymas the sorcerer, "Behold, the hand of the Lord is upon thee, and thou shalt be blind, not seeing the sun for a season" and "a mist and a darkness" immediately fell upon him.

So I "blinded" the customs agent in Jesus' name. What happened? I don't know. God had told me to blind him, so I know he was blind; but I do not think he was physically blind—I think he was spiritually blind. He did not discern that the book he was looking at was the Word of God, even though he could read

English perfectly well, as I had seen when he read my passport.

He took my Bible out and began to thumb through it. Turning his head towards me and looking straight in my eyes, he said, "Do you have any more books?"

I had books—Bibles—in every pocket. I was loaded with the unadulterated Word of the Living God. I said yes. I felt like I was literally growing taller. A supernatural boldness and power came upon me, and again I "blinded" his eyes in Jesus' name. I didn't know exactly what would happen, but I did know God had intervened.

The man looked in the middle compartment of my brown bag and found another Bible. Then he turned to me, paused a moment, and shoved my bag and Bibles back to me with an order to move on. God had not allowed him to read, *"Holy Bible"* on the bindings of the books. Since then, I have carried many Gospels through Russian customs untouched, unsearched and unquestioned. Hallelujah!

Romans 8:6 says, "For to be carnally [naturally or fleshly] minded is death; but to be spiritually minded [have the mind of the Spirit] is life and peace." Verse 7 continues, "Because the carnal mind [mind of the flesh] is enmity against God: for it is not subject to the law of God, neither indeed can be." It does matter what you allow to enter your mind. This is the very hour in history that one must watch and scrutinize every thought that seeks entrance to keep out the trash of this world.

We need to understand that there is always a negative and a positive. A carnal or natural mind that entertains natural thoughts can only live in a realm of death. Why? Because the Bible says, "For to be carnally [naturally] minded produces death; but to be spiritually minded [produces] life and peace."

As I mentioned before, my good friend asked me why he had no peace of mind—why he took the stand of faith and nothing happened. At times when you get no answer or only a partial answer something is wrong. And I'll tell you what that "something" is. You have been thinking wrong! You have allowed the thoughts put there by the devil to gain strongholds in your mind. When negative thoughts have come, you have allowed them to dwell in your mind.

Someone once said, "It is no sin for birds to fly over your head, but you don't have to let them nest in your hair." Negative thoughts are Satan's lies. He comes and speaks a "reasonable" sounding word of doubt to you. That produces a thought. If you let that thought "nest"—if you entertain that negative thought even though it is contrary to God's Word—it will come to dwell in your mind till you think it is your own. Then it will flow into your spirit till your very heart and soul are filled with that thought. Eventually, you will not only be thinking wrong thoughts, but you will be speaking wrong words. As it says in Matthew 12:34, "out of the abundance of the heart [human spirit] the mouth speaketh."

People get into the habit of letting their thoughts dwell on their weaknesses and failures. Then their thinking turns a momentary setback into out-and-out defeat. They express their "lack of faith," and that increases their doubt. What you think in your heart goes down into your spirit, and when that happens, "out of the abundance of the heart the mouth speaketh."

It matters what you say. The Bible says, "Who so ever ... shall not doubt in his heart ... he shall have what so ever he *saith*."

You think, "I'm going to lose my business," and that is what you say to yourself over and over until it comes to pass.

You think, "I'm going to die of this sickness," and death can be the result of your fear-thought.

When you think negative thoughts, you get negative responses.

When you think fear, fear grips you.

When you think disaster, disaster grabs you.

When you think bankruptcy, bankruptcy trips you.

When you think failure, failure trails you.

Notice the progression from thoughts, to words, to deeds, to consequences. This progression occurs in the positive realm as well as the negative.

You get what you think. Do you want to know how to think right? The whole solution is so simple it's easy to miss it. The Bible says, "For as [a man] thinketh in his heart [or spirit], so is he" (Proverbs 23:7). Don't *allow* negative thoughts—which are really the lies of Satan—to oppose the Word of God, "neither give place to the devil" (Ephesians 4:27); "but to be spiritually minded is life and peace" (Romans 8:6).

Casting Down Thoughts

"For though we walk in the flesh, we do not war after the flesh: (For the weapons of our warfare are not carnal [of the flesh], but mighty through God to the pulling down of strong holds;) Casting down imaginations, and every high thing that exalteth itself against the knowledge of God, and bringing into captivity every thought to the obedience of Christ;" (2 Corinthians 10:3-5).

Under all circumstances and at all times, train yourself to think as God thinks. Diligently learn how to put on the mind of Christ. "Let this mind be in you, which was also in Christ Jesus" (Philippians 2:5).

God has called us to "Fight the good fight of faith, lay hold on eternal life, whereunto thou art also called, and hast professed a good profession before many witnesses" (1 Timothy 6:12).

In the fight of faith, there is but one weapon—the Word of God. The combat is with the thoughts in the mind. Therefore, put on the mind of Christ. How? We must put our minds in God's Word. Only God's Word in our minds will cast down negative thoughts. As we put our mind on God's Word and richly meditate and dwell on it instead of on negative thoughts, the mind of Christ is being put on, even "when the enemy shall come in like a flood" (Isaiah 59:19).

As we put on the mind of Christ daily, "the Spirit of the Lord shall lift up a standard against the enemy" (Isaiah 59:19).

When thoughts of frustration fill your mind and you have no peace, put on the mind of Christ daily. "Great peace have they which love thy law" (Psalm 119:165).

Put on the mind of Christ daily because, "Thou wilt keep him in perfect peace, whose mind is stayed on thee" (Isaiah 26:3).

Learn to put on the mind of Christ daily, "And the peace of God which passeth all understanding, shall keep your hearts [spirits] and minds through Christ Jesus" (Philippians 4:7).

Learn to put on the mind of Christ daily because Jesus said, "Peace I leave with you, my peace I give unto you: not as the world giveth, give I unto you. Let not your heart be troubled, neither let it be afraid" (John 14:27).

Let these words sink deep down into your heart, and you will get positive results daily.

When thoughts of fear try to fill your mind, put on the mind of Christ, because "the Lord is the strength of my life; of whom shall I be afraid?" (Psalm 27:1). "Thou shalt not be afraid for the terror by night; nor for the arrow that flieth by day" (Psalm 91:5). "Fear thou not; for I am with thee: be not dismayed; for I am thy God" (Isaiah 41:10).

Memorizing and learning these verses, as well as thinking upon them at length until they become welded to your spirit, will be enable you to "let this mind be in you, which also was in Christ Jesus." Put on the mind of Christ daily.

When sickness, or death, or poverty strikes, quote the words of the Bible which fit that circumstance as a means of putting on the mind of Christ.

When trouble strikes, use "It is God that girdeth me with strength, and maketh my way perfect" (Psalm 18:32).

When illness strikes, or disease cripples, dwell in "With His stripes we are healed" (Isaiah 53:5), and also "[He] healeth all thy diseases" (Psalm 103:3). Then there is Exodus 15:26, "I am the Lord that healeth thee." Matthew 8:17 confirms the words of the prophet Isaiah when it quotes, "Himself took our infirmities, and bare our sicknesses."

As these words become a part of your very being, they will change you in the innermost reaches of your mind and spirit and cause you to become a new creation in Christ Jesus because you have truly put on the mind of Christ.

When poverty comes, either through loss of job or through other disaster, put on what God's Word has to say about that. "But my God shall supply all your need according to his riches in glory by Christ Jesus" (Phillippians 4:19).

"The thoughts of the diligent tend only to plenteousness" (Proverbs 21:5). We can also claim, "The wealth of the sinner is laid up for the just" (Proverbs 13:22). It is heartening to recall, "But thou shalt remember the Lord thy God: for it is he that giveth thee power to get wealth" (Deuteronomy 8:18).

Finally, brethren, whatsoever things are true,
whatsoever things are honest,
whatsoever things are just,
whatsoever things are pure,
whatsoever things are lovely,
whatsoever things are of good report:

if there be any virtue, and if there be any praise, think on these things" (Philippians 4:8).

Let These Words Sink Into Your Heart

When you use the Word negatively, it tends to bring forth death instead of life. But when you use the Word of God to take the place of any sin (lying, doubts, sickness, poverty, thoughts of adultery, any work of Satan that would exalt itself against God), then you are putting on the *Mind of Christ.* It becomes a ministry of life, and of well-being, and well-doing.

In Proverbs 23:7, the Holy Spirit reveals, "For as [a man] thinketh in his heart, so is he." When we put on the mind of Christ, we stand in a place where we can behold the miraculous works of God!

Putting on the Mind of Christ Brings Victory in Czechoslovakia

The Word of God is power over all the powers of the enemy. The Bible, God's Word, is the total, complete authority over all of the power of the enemy! "Heaven and earth shall pass away, but my words shall not pass away" (Matthew 24:35). I may pass away, you may pass away, but the Word of God stands sure— it will never pass away. Hallelujah!

By the power of God I have often passed safely through Russian customs, in spite of the Bibles I was carrying. I have risked my life many times in this manner. I have had visions of God. Three times I have been transported in the Spirit. I have had all kinds of supernatural experiences in the power of the Holy Spirit. But in Czechoslovakia, God showed me a new vista—another avenue to victory. "As many as are led by the Spirit of God, they are the sons of God" (Romans 8:14).

When I was in Czechoslovakia, the weather was atrocious—simply terrible. The temperature was six degrees below zero, and it was snowing. I had no idea where I could go to find Christians who needed the Bibles I was carrying. At that low moment God spoke to me, saying, "Son, be of good cheer. You are going to take these Gospels to the right place." As He spoke, He showed me a vision of a two-story house.

I hailed a taxicab and climbed in. When the driver asked me where I was going, I told him that I wasn't quite sure but that I would direct him street by street.

Do you know what happened? We came to a corner. With the Holy Spirit guiding me, I told the driver to turn right, then to go to the next corner and turn left. Then I instructed the driver to stop. There it was—the same two-story house the Lord had shown me in the vision. It was a miracle taking place right before my eyes. God had given me perfect directions!

The Word of God had seemed to flow into my mind. I had pictured the place before we got there, and it had looked exactly the way I had seen it! The Holy Spirit had gone before me to make the crooked places straight!

I had proceeded as the Holy Spirit directed—and yet for a moment I was attacked by doubt.

I got out of the cab and went alone up the steps. At the top I stopped and knocked on the door, just as though I were knocking on the door of my best friend.

A lady came to the door and spoke to me in Slovak, a language I do not understand. As she spoke, the door seemed to swing open of its own accord until the whole room was in view. Then, automatically, before I realized what I was saying, I cried, "Hallelujah!" She looked at me quizzically and jumped back a bit. Then I saw behind her two Russian soldiers in full uniform with red stars shining on their shoulders. They were sitting on a cot.

All kinds of thoughts raced through my mind. I was attacked by a demonic spirit of fear. Like a bolt of lightning, it drove into the deep recesses of my heart. It was so strong the pit of my stomach tensed up. Cold chills ran from the crown of my head to the soles of my feet.

These unexpected circumstances created thoughts full of fear, thoughts straight from the devil. Then the devil said, "Now you've walked into a trap. You're going to be arrested."

But I had learned to cast down all imaginations and strongholds that exalt themselves against the Word of God. Determinedly I put on the mind of Christ.

Way down in the innermost recesses of my being, the Holy Spirit began to rise up. As the Holy Spirit whispered His Words to me, they renewed my thinking. I heard the Voice of the Holy Spirit saying, "Chris Panos, fear thou not; for I am with thee: be not dismayed; for I am thy God: I will strengthen thee; yea, I will help thee; yea, I will uphold thee with the right hand of my righteousness" (Isaiah 41:10).

Praise the Lord! No matter what the circumstances, I could stand there well and strong in spirit and mind. I didn't know what to do about the soldiers. (I wasn't quite sure yet whether to bind them, or to blind them.) But it didn't matter. I have learned to put on the mind of Christ, and that's what I did. "Behold I give unto you power ... over all the power of the enemy" (Luke 10:19). Whenever I am in doubt, I always bind the enemy in the name of Jesus.

As I stood there, the Holy Spirit renewed my mind because I had learned the secret of putting on the mind of Christ. When you can put on the mind of Christ, "No weapon that is formed against [you] shall prosper" (Isaiah 54:17). There is power in the name of Jesus! "God hath not given us the spirit of fear; but of power, and of love, and of a sound mind" (2 Timothy 1:7).

As I said, "Hallelujah," I was amazed as the lady at the door replied, "Hallelujah." So again I said, "Hallelujah." She replied, "Hallelujah." Then I inquired, "Do you speak English?"

Again she rejoiced, "Hallelujah!"

Well, praise the Lord! We were having a hallelujah time! However, nobody could speak English. But God had led me to say the word that is the same in all languages—hallelujah—and that broke the language barrier! There are absolutely no closed doors to the Gospel, the power of God unto salvation.

The lady motioned that I should come on into the house since it was so bitterly cold. Moved by the Holy

Spirit, I motioned to ask her if she had a son, and if she would get him.

I still didn't know what was going to happen next. But oh, how sweet it is, how wonderful, to hear that still, sweet, small Voice of Jesus when you've gone as far as you can. When you're in a Communist nation, it's not hard to be really consecrated! It's not difficult to pray. It's easy to get hold of God, and to pray all night in a country where almost everybody is an unbeliever and a Communist—you're afraid not to!

In just a moment, the lady's son came into the room. I signaled to him that we needed an interpreter. He nodded his understanding, went out, and brought back with him the village school teacher.

While they were away and I waited quietly, the Holy Spirit reassured me that I should give the Russian soldiers a Bible. When I could, I told them I had come to bring Good News. I handed them the two Russian Bibles which I produced for that purpose. When they saw what they had, a smile broke over their faces and they began to weep tears of joy.

They opened the Bible and began to read John 3:16, "God so loved the world, that he gave his only begotten Son, that whosoever believeth in Him should not perish, but have everlasting life." These Russian soldiers had never been saved, but they were very tender toward Christianity. They had been led by the Holy Spirit to the home of this Slovak family where God knew they would receive the Gospel of Jesus Christ!

CHAPTER 3

WHAT YOU SAY IS WHAT YOU GET

Some of you are puzzled. You ask, "Why am I faced with this sickness?" "Why has this disease come against my family?" "Why do these financial mountains block my way to success?" "Why is my child doing this or that?"

It seems that some unseen force fills the air around you with fear. "Why do I feel depressed, and why is everything in the world happening to me?" Many of you who read these lines today are in desperate need of a miracle answer. You need to know once and for all what is the matter with your ministry, your business, your family, your surroundings. You yearn for a miracle that will usher you through these hard places into the fullness of the blessings of the Lord.

Thank God, I have good news for you! You can have God's miraculous faith, which will blast you through the pressing need that faces you. You can have a miracle, because God is a miracle-working God. There are many infallible proofs of His miracles recorded in the Bible.

Let your eyes behold our miracle-working God as we read some scriptures together and I share with you some unusual experiences that happened to me in Red Communist countries.

I want to call your attention to a pattern of victory outlined in these scriptures: "Jesus Christ [is] the same yesterday, and to day, and forever" (Hebrews 13:8). "For verily I say unto you, That whosoever shall say unto this mountain, Be thou removed.... and shall not doubt in his heart, but shall believe that those things which he saith shall come to pass; he shall have whatsoever he saith" (Mark 11:23). "The word is nigh thee, even in thy mouth, and in thy heart: that is, the word of faith, which we preach [or say, or speak]" (Romans 10:8). "Samuel grew, and the LORD was with him, and did let none of his words fall to the ground" (1 Samuel 3:19). What a place to be with God!

Say What God Says

It *is* important what you say (speak or confess). Many people fail to receive what they pray for because they do not understand the power the Lord has invested in *confession*.

In Hebrews 3:1, the whole of Christianity is called a "confession." (The Greek word here translated in the King James Version as "profession" is the same Greek word usually translated "confession.") Whenever the word "confession" is used, automatically one thinks of confessing sin, weakness and failure. But this is only the negative side of the subject.

The negative confession of our sin is intended only to open the way to the positive confession of God's Word. The word "confession" in Greek could as easily be translated, "saying the same thing." It means to believe and to say the same thing that God says about our sins, our sicknesses, our financial needs, and everything else included in our redemption.

Our confession is simply our affirmation of Bible truth. It is simply believing with our hearts and repeating with our lips God's own declaration of what we are in Christ.

Jesus said, "Whosoever shall say unto this mountain, Be thou removed, and be thou cast into the sea; and shall not doubt in his heart, but shall believe that those things which he saith shall come to pass; he shall have whatsoever he saith" (Mark 11:23). When we say what God says, that is not telling a lie.

If you need finances, say what God says. Don't repeat the negative reality that you need finances. Affirm that "My God shall supply all your need according to his riches in glory by Christ Jesus" (Philipians 4:19).

Under all circumstances and at all times, speak and affirm God's Word. Train yourself to be pleasing to God in your way of life and manner of speech. His attitude, as set forth in the Word, will be developed into your life until Satan cannot prevail against you. God's Word will become molded into your very life and nature. You will become irresistible as God is irresistible, because God's Word of faith in your heart will come to control your prayers, your words, your thoughts, and your actions.

Confession has several aspects. It is speaking what God says in and about every situation of your life at all times. It is resisting Satan with a "thus saith the Lord" to overthrow the roadblocks he has set up to thwart God's purposes in your life. It is claiming your rights at the Throne of Grace, confessing God's promises: "For though we walk in the flesh, we do not war after the flesh: (For the weapons of our warfare are not carnal [of the flesh], but mighty through God to the pulling down of strongholds)" (2 Corinthians 10:3-4). It cannot be reiterated too strongly that the Greek word from which "confession" is translated means "saying the same thing"—saying what God says—*agreeing with God in our conversation.*

In 1 Peter 2:24, the Holy Spirit says, "By whose stripes ye were healed." We are to believe and to say the same things that God says.

God watches over His Word to make it good. The Lord says, "I am alert and active, watching over My word to perform it" (Jeremiah 1:12, Amplified).

If it's finances, then "The Lord is my shepherd; I shall not want" (Psalm 23:1). Confession is faith's way of expressing itself.

Our faith (or unbelief) is determined by our confession. Few realize the effect of the spoken word on our own heart, or on our adversary.

Satan hears the confession of our failure, of sickness, and of lack, and he brings us down to the level of our confession. No one ever rises above the level of his confession.

If you confess sickness, a stronghold of sickness is developed in your system. If you confess doubt, the walls of doubt are stacked stronger and higher. If you confess your lack of finances, it stops money from coming in.

If you say, "I can't understand this," then you cannot understand it. You were snared by what you said. Always remember that the words we speak germinate the atmosphere around us.

Dare to Speak Out

St. Paul tells us that he preached "the word of faith." Out of his mouth comes the timeless principle: "That if thou shalt confess with thy mouth the Lord Jesus, and shalt believe in thine heart that God hath raised Him from the dead, thou shalt be saved. For with the heart man believeth unto righteousness; and with the mouth confession is made unto salvation" (Romans 10:9-10).

The words we speak generate the atmosphere around us. To generate a victorious atmosphere, open your mouth and *speak* the word of God. "The word is . . . in thy mouth, and in thy heart: that is, the word of faith, which we preach" (Romans 10:8).

One time when I was in Moscow, I had gone down to the restaurant to get something to eat. When I walked in, there was only one table available. It was in the center of the restaurant.

In Russia, the custom is that the first person who sits down at a table has the authority to give permission for others to sit with him. An English couple walked up and asked permission to sit at my table. I responded,

"Please do." They sat down. Then a Russian lady came along. She asked if she could share the table. I said, "Please do."

She began to talk immediately: "I teach a class of six-year-olds. I teach them of our great father Lenin." She continued to talk about what a great deliverer Lenin was, and how he delivered Russia from capitalism and from the Czar, giving the Russians real freedom. Those were her words. That was her confession. She spoke with authority and she was convincing.

But way down in the inner recesses of my being, there was righteous indignation. A powerful anger mixed with divine love rose up in me. I said to her, "My dear lady, Lenin was not the deliverer. Jesus Christ is the Deliverer of all mankind, including Russia." That was *my* confession.

She asked, "What do you do?"

I said, "I'm also a teacher. I teach that 'God so loved the world, that he gave his only begotten Son, that whosoever believeth in him should not perish, but have everlasting life' " (John 3:16).

This Russian teacher spoke many words and they were "positive" words. I spoke many words, and they were words of faith. She became furious as I continued to talk about the shed blood of Jesus Christ and the cross. I said, "The blood of Jesus Christ . . . cleanseth us from all unrighteousness!"

She couldn't combat these powerful spoken words any longer. She arose angrily and stamped her foot, shouting, "Lenin is the only deliverer!" Then she whirled around. Her high heels beat an enraged staccato as she stomped off.

Words! Just words and more words. But *her* words

fell to the ground and passed away, because they were only natural words.

My words were God's words, "quick, and powerful, and sharper than any two-edged sword" (Hebrews 4:12). Yes, there is power in God's Word! Not one of His words fell to the ground and perished!

Instead they fell on good ground, straight into the heart of the young Englishwoman who was sitting on my right. Her eyes flooded with tears, then tears were streaming down her face: "If you love this Jesus so much you would risk your life to tell His story, then I want this Jesus to come and live in my heart. I want Jesus now. I want to receive Jesus Christ as my Savior. I want His blood to cleanse my heart right now."

In a few moments that Englishwoman received Jesus Christ as Lord and Savior. She was born again. Praise the Lord!

That's the power of God's Word, when you speak it out.

His Word will generate the presence of Jesus Christ! God watches over His Word to perform it.

God's promises are in your mouth.

Dare to say them!

Dare to confess them!

They will generate the presence of Jesus Christ in your heart and life.

"The word is nigh thee, even in thy mouth, and in thine heart."

That is the word of faith which we preach, which we say! Say faith words to yourself. Say them to those who oppose you, as I did to the woman who was a Russian informer. Say them to the devil! Say them to sickness! Say them to your mountain of trouble! Say them in the face of all contrary evidence! Say them while the pain is there! Say them to financial needs. Your faith words will generate victory!

"Let the weak say, I am strong" (Joel 3:10).

As you speak, God is looking down saying (in effect), "That's My little boy, My little girl, speaking My words."

The Bible says: "Whosoever shall say unto this mountain, Be thou removed, and be thou cast into the sea; and shall not doubt in his heart, but shall believe that those things which he saith shall come to pass; he shall have whatsoever he saith" (Mark 11:24). Praise the Lord!

What We Say Will Happen

Notice here that our confession (saying the same thing that God says) is *by faith*—that is, believing and confessing *before* experiencing the result.

Confession comes first; and then Jesus, our High Priest, responds with His answer in His mercy and grace. (The lady from England was saved in Russia by hearing the spoken *Word* of God.)

It is not salvation unto confession, but confession unto salvation. Confession must come before salvation.

There is no such thing as salvation without confession. Faith is acting upon God's Word. And this always moves God to work and to fulfill His Promise.

Confession unto salvation is the initial blessing. First

38

comes the new birth, and then one is eligible to claim every blessing promised in the Word of God to believers. Abraham was a Gentile when he heard and heeded the call of God to "Get thee out of thy country, and from thy kindred, and from thy father's house, unto a land that I will shew thee" (Genesis 12:1). Hebrews 11:10 says, "He looked for a city which hath foundations, whose builder and maker is God."

If fear strikes you, say God's Word aloud, "Be not afraid, only believe" (Mark 5:36).

If finances drop and you are in need, say God's Word, "Yea, the Almighty shall be thy defence, and thou shalt have plenty of silver" (Job 22:25).

If sickness strikes you or your family, say God's Word about Jesus, "By whose stripes ye were healed" (1 Peter 2:24).

If there are trials and afflictions, say God's Word, "Many are the afflictions of the righteous: but the Lord delivereth him out of them all" (Psalm 34:19).

The Christian is to act on every phase of his salvation as soon as the Lord reveals it to him. We are to believe with the heart and confess with our mouth to the extent of the "Word of Faith" which Paul preached. "For with the heart man believeth unto righteousness; and with the mouth confession is made unto salvation" (Romans 10:10).

Paul preached "all the counsel of God" (Acts 20:27).

He preached "the unsearchable riches of Christ" (Ephesians 3:8).

He said that he "kept back nothing that was profitable" (Acts 20:20).

There are salvation words of God in your mouth!

There are miracle words of God in your mouth!

There are healing words of God in your mouth!

There are prosperity words of God in your mouth!

SPEAK THEM! SAY THEM! CONFESS THEM!

The words you speak either generate the presence and power of God, or they generate defeat. What kind of words are you speaking? Listen very carefully to this next statement—

All that Jesus did for us on the cross belongs to us. So, throughout our Christian life, God wants us to believe with our heart and say with our lips all He says we are in Christ.

We are to confess (to say, to whisper in our own heart), "Ye are complete in him" (Colossians 2:10).

When we know that God in His Word says, "I am the LORD that healeth thee" (Exodus 15:26), we are to believe it and confess it—say it with our lips—and it will come to pass.

WE ARE TO CONFESS THAT CALVARY (THE CROSS) IS OUR DELIVERANCE FROM EVERYTHING OUTSIDE OF THE WILL OF GOD FOR OUR LIVES. THEN WE ARE TO ACT LIKE WE MEAN IT AS WE SPEAK.

We are to confess that our sickness, our financial problem, our family problem, our sorrow, and our pain were laid on Christ. "CHRIST HATH REDEEMED US FROM THE CURSE OF THE LAW" (Galatians 3:13). The curse of the law is SIN-SICKNESS-DISEASE-POVERTY. "Let the weak say, I am strong"

(Joel 3:10); "For the Lord Jehovah is my strength" (Isaiah 12:2).

We are to confess that our redemption is complete. Satan's dominion is ended. The cross has freed us. "Whosoever believeth in him [Jesus] shall receive remission of sins" (Acts 10:43).

"Remission of sins" is the wiping away of everything connected with the old life. The dictionary says that to remit is to "release from the guilt or penalty of." We are to say what God says. What we confess today, we possess tomorrow—whether good or bad, sickness or health, poverty or wealth, weakness or power to evangelize the world.

Hold Fast Your Confession

Hebrews 4:14 says, "Seeing then we have a great High Priest, that is passed into the heavens, Jesus the Son of God, let us hold fast our profession [confession]." The confession of our faith, then, is the redemptive work that God wrought in Christ "to present you faultless before the presence of his glory with exceeding joy" (Jude 1:24).

I am told to hold fast my confession of the Word of God!

I am told to hold fast to the confession that "the Lord is the strength of my life" (Psalm 27:1).

I am told to hold fast the confession that "surely He hath borne our griefs and carried our sorrows.... and with his stripes we are healed" (Isaiah 53:4-5).

41

God says these things in His Word. We are to declare the same things God says.

When you know that Christ "took our infirmities and bare our sicknesses" (Matthew 8:17), hold fast to your confession of it.

When you know that "greater is he that is in you, than he that is in the world" (1 John 4:4), hold fast to your confession of it.

When you know that "the blessing of the Lord, it maketh rich, and he addeth no sorrow with it" (Proverbs 10:22), hold fast to your confession of it! We are to hold fast to our confession in the face of all seeming "evidence" to the contrary.

God declares that "with his stripes we are healed" (Isaiah 53:5).

I am to say what God says about my sickness and to hold fast to His confession.

I am to recognize the absolute truthfulness of these words even *before* any visible change is seen.

I am to act on these words, and to thank Him for the fact that He laid my sicknesses on Christ in the same way as He did my sins.

Miracle Words of Faith

The confession of your lips that has grown out of faith in your heart will absolutely defeat our adversary, the devil, in every combat.

Christ's words broke the power of demons and healed the sick. We must speak death-defying, devil-defeating words; for we have the keys to the kingdom—

God's Word. Jesus said, "Behold I give you power . . . over all the power of the enemy" (Luke 10:19). "For this purpose the Son of God was manifested, that he might destroy the works of the devil" (1 John 3:8).

Miracle Weather From Miracle Words

There was an outstanding incident during the crusade in Prodattur, India. The rain clouds always rose up in great force and number just before time for the meetings. The clouds always seemed to be the blackest over the crusade grounds. One night the rain was falling hard ten minutes before time to start the crusade. When I arrived at the grounds, a powerful force of God gripped me as I went to the microphone. I began to speak the miracle words of God that rose up within my spirit.

I went to the microphone and began binding the dark clouds with the Word of God. I commanded the dark clouds over the crusade grounds to leave.

Then the rain stopped.

Then I commanded the clouds to obey the resurrected words of God that said "Behold I give you power . . . over all the power of the enemy" (Luke 10:19).

I shouted, "Go! In Jesus Christ's name, leave these grounds now." Immediately the clouds left as though a mighty wind had swept them away.

It was a host of unseen angels who formed a protective circle around the crusade grounds and forbade the rain to enter. It was still raining hard all around this circle of angels, but over the crusade grounds not one drop was falling. Around the grounds many clouds still surrounded the adjacent area, but over the grounds where our lights were, and where people were standing, there were no clouds nor was there any rain. It was "off limits" for any clouds to rain on those crusade grounds. Praise be unto God!

"Jesus Christ the same yesterday, and today and forever" (Hebrews 13:8). The words of Jesus have the same power today when we believe them and say them. The Word of God will move clouds, move mountains, move financial problems, and move crises out of your family. Jesus' words are able to move all circumstances and to change the destiny of your life. They can move your sickness and give an answer to your every problem. If you continually confess the Word of God, God will make your body obey your confession of His Word and will change the circumstances, because "No word of God is void of power" (Luke 1:37, alternate reading). The words you speak germinate the atmosphere around you.

Faith comes as the word that we hear flows from our lips and produces miracles.

It is not our faith; it is God's Word working in our hearts. The Word quickens, growing in power until it sets your very soul aflame.

This kind of faith makes all things possible as we speak God's Word (say it and confess it).

Nothing will establish you and build your faith as quickly as confession of His Word. God says, "It [the Word] shall not return unto me void!"

There is power in the Word of God. There is power in the words of Jesus. Jesus said, "The words that I speak unto you, they are spirit, and they are life" (John 6:63).

Jesus Christ spoke words of life into the tomb of Lazarus where he lay dead. The life of God's power went into that tomb and Lazarus's body was unshackled from the bonds of death. The divine life of faith words flowed into that tomb and Lazarus was resurrected.

There is *power* in God's words.

The Bible says that the religious leaders of that day spoke of the power and authority with which Jesus spoke. They were astonished at His doctrine.

"And they were all amazed, insomuch that they questioned among themselves, saying, What thing is this? What new doctrine is this? for with authority commandeth he even the unclean spirits, and they do obey him" (Mark 1:27).

Jesus' words had power. He commanded the unclean spirits to come out—and the unclean spirits obeyed His words. There was power in the words of Jesus 2,000 years ago.

There is power in God's words. God works through us by His words through our lips.

Jesus said, "Go teach." We carry the Word, and if we don't give out the Word, we don't do anything. You're wasting your time praying that God will do something. If someone is lost, you would be wasting your time praying for God to save him unless someone carries the Word to him.

Let there be a daily confession in your life of the Word of God *in your mouth.* It is the Word of God in your lips that counts. The Word becomes a living thing in the lips of the believer. It brings salvation to the sinner.

Your word becomes God's Word as you speak His Word. God's miracle words for salvation are in your mouth. God's Word to perform miracles is in your mouth. God's Word to bring healing is in your mouth.

Let the unsaved say, "Save me, and I shall be saved" (Jeremiah 17:14).

Let the weak say, "I am strong" (Joel 3:10).

Let the sick say, "By His stripes we are healed" (Isaiah 53:5).

Let the sick say, "By his stripes we are healed" (Isaiah 53:5).

Every day I take these words, *His* words to God. I pray for the people connected with my ministry. I speak scriptures for salvation, scriptures for healing, scriptures for miracles, scriptures for finances, and scriptures for praise.

Miracle faith words flow from my lips daily. I affirm daily that I have new power. "Behold I give unto you power to tread on serpents and scorpions, and over all the power of the enemy: and nothing shall by any means hurt you" (Luke 10:19).

I say daily, "I am healed by His stripes" (Isaiah 53:5).

I say daily, "But my God shall supply all my need" (Philippians 4:19).

I say daily, "No weapon that is formed against [me] shall prosper" (Isaiah 54:17).

I say daily, "Though I walk through the valley of the shadow of death, I will fear no evil" (Psalm 23:4).

I say daily, "God hath not given us the spirit of fear; but of power, and of love, and of a sound mind" (2 Timothy 1:7).

I say daily, "Thank You Father, that I am prospering

and I am a success, because the Bible says my "delight is in the law of the Lord: and in His law doth he meditate day and night. And he shall be like a tree planted by the rivers of waters ... his leaf also shall not wither; and whatsoever he doeth shall prosper" (Psalm 1:1-3).

We speak daily these words of prayer and praise for all our directors and Far East Reporter family.

Say what God says, and you will live a victorious Christian life.

I want to say to you that your life has been changed through the word which you have read; it is in the process of changing again and again from glory to glory (2 Corinthians 3:18) as we continue our journey together through the pages of this book.

CHAPTER 4

THE WAY OF FAITH

How helpless is man to cope with present conditions! How futile are our efforts and how weak is the arm of flesh! A thousand times in human history the announcement has been made by triumphant armies that peace has come at last; but with the passing of a few years at the most, the conflict breaks out all over again and the feeble and futile efforts of man to bring about peace without God result each time in only the breaking down of existing systems.

Peace is something more than just words. It is something more than the silencing of the guns. Because the soldiers of the nations change their clothes does not of necessity mean that they change their hearts and minds. How I wish I had a voice that would reach to the uttermost parts of the earth to herald the tidings that it is "Not by might nor by power, but by my spirit, saith the

LORD" that the things for which we have been striving will in reality be brought about.

Religious systems may have failed, but Jesus is still the Victor. They may stand unclothed in the midst of their appalling helplessness, but CHRIST STILL REIGNS. When, oh, when will this world realize that it is not by military might nor by the power of the human mind or the intellect, but by the spirit of the Lord that the things for which we strive will be brought about?

The Lord has been speaking to my heart about the power of faith as I have waited before Him. As I have read His precious Word, and particularly as the unfolding revelation of the Holy Spirit has come to me, I have become more and more convinced of the absolute helplessness of man unless he is animated and activated by the Holy Spirit.

It is only when we become a channel through which the Word of the Lord can flow and the manifestation of the divine indwelling can be demonstrated according to the divine will, that what we call our ministry is acceptable in the sight of the Lord. Knowing our human tendencies to exalt self and enthrone the flesh, the Lord chose the weak, the despised, and the base things as the means and media through which He would reveal Himself and His Word, in order that no flesh should glory in His presence.

No empty definition can reveal Jesus! Even though our doctrines be true, they are not the purveyors of the manifestations of His power. Our Heavenly Father is wanting us to move out of the abstract realm in which we take pride in our orthodoxy and our understanding of the printed word, into the place where the Word will again become living reality and dwell among us; and once more we shall behold His glory as the only begotten of the Father.

We are living in an hour when our Lord would translate us from the place where we had to keep our feet on the ground and indulge in platitudes, beautiful theories, and sweet sentiments into that higher realm where we shall actually experience the omnipotence of God's faith and the full recognition of our identification with Jesus as our heritage.

Where Are The Men of Faith?

Let us face the issue. Confession is important, but have we really *possessed* what we have confessed? Where are the "greater things" of which Jesus spoke to His disciples in days long ago? What have we done with His promise that *whatsoever we should ask in His name that He would do?* Where is the manifestation of the mountain-moving faith which He made available to His followers in the wonderful statement He made by the side of the shriveled, dried-up fig tree? What has become of the signs which were to follow them that believe?

These things were not to be the ministry of angels, but they were to be the ministry of men. They were not reserved for the day when time should be no more and we would be safely home in our Father's house of many mansions. They were to be possessed by His Church, and the gates of hell were not to prevail against it.

God's children were to be the possessors of a faith that would spread tables in the wilderness and turn the desert into springs of water.

They were to be the channel through which the dynamic God would come in such irresistable power that kingdoms would be subdued and the works of righteousness would be manifest!

The mouths of lions were to be stopped!

And this omnipotent faith would deliver from the edge of the sword—yes, spiritual weaklings were to be turned into warriors.

His Mantle

The world has stood in gaping wonder because science has split the atom and given us the A-Bomb and the H-Bomb, and even sent man into outer space to land on the moon; but little do they know that there is an explosive, irresistible, omnipotent power in faith that ought to make the atomic bomb and reaching the moon look like child's play! One day Jesus helped us see the faith of God in its irresistible, explosive, dynamic power; and He so portrayed it that He took the word "impossible" out of the dictionary of the "hundred-fold" Christian when He said, "With men this is impossible, But with God *all things* are possible!" (Matthew 19:26).

Now please do not make the mistake we have been making through the years in misinterpreting the preposition. We have been saying, "Yes, I believe that, all things are possible *to* God." Now we know that all things are possible *to* God, but that is not what the Scripture says in this instance; and the direct declaration of Jesus is proof conclusive that He is not talking about the power of God apart from man. He is talking about the power of God working in and through man, in other words, our working *with* Him.

We have been inclined to shrug our shoulders and say, "Well, this cannot be done, with man this thing is impossible. Only God could do it." There is a sense in which that is true, but it is not the message Jesus gave to His listeners on that tremendous day. To say that He meant man must stand apart from God, in recognition of His omnipotence, is all right as far as it goes; but it does not go far enough. That is just what we have done. We have assumed that the impossible would be accomplished *for* man and not *by* man. What Jesus meant was that the weakness of man could be linked with the strength of God, of the omnipotent God, and that this union would make him strong in the strength which God supplies through His Eternal Son. It meant that God would manifest Himself *through* man and not merely on his behalf. Too, it meant that man can receive into his own spirit the very energy and power of Almighty God. Then the faith that laughs at impossibilities would begin to operate in and through the surrendered, yielded, consecrated heart in God's new creation.

God Does It

Unless God does it, we cannot do it. It is of no use to try. We can rebuke and shout and carry on, forgetting all the while that the prophets of Baal did that very thing. They shouted, but it brought no power and there was no manifestation of fire. They probably were sincere, but even that did them no good. They were very religious, but that did not help. They even went so far as to mortify the flesh by cutting themselves with knives and lancers, but it was all to no avail.

Among all the preachers on the summit of Mt. Carmel that day, there was only one who had visualized the truth, only one mind which had been so touched by the Divine that it saw through all the follies of idol worship into the great Eternal realms of Divine Truth and recognized the omnipotent God.

Elijah knew that flesh could never perform the miracle. He knew that God alone was able and *willing* to catch the prayer of the man who had entered into oneness with Him, and send the fire down. And what fire it was! It not only burned up the wood, but it consumed stones as if they were kindling, and water as though it were gasoline.

Now, it is of no use to climb up some Carmel unless God leads you up the mountainside. In the last analysis, we are foolish to move unless we are led by the Spirit. I am one man who actually believes that we can live the Spirit-led, Spirit-directed life. It is not enough to run around commanding here and rebuking there. Unless God is leading, we will go away defeated and humiliated over and over again, as in the past. We will know in our hearts that something is wrong—but what? Is it not that our Heavenly Father is trying to teach us to "have God's faith"?

Faith Cometh

"Now faith *cometh*" (Romans 10:17; italics added). It is not generated in the human mind. It is not manufactured in the intellect, nor is it manufactured in the minds of reason. Neither can it be produced by the sentiments of the heart, or by "positive thinking." Man can no more possess faith in himself—and by himself—than he can possess grace apart from God. Is it possible for us to have the love of God without having God Himself produce and give us that love? If the human personality were capable of generating a love which would be equal to the love of God, it still would not be God's love, it would be ours. Listen to me very carefully: *Man never discovers God's strength until he first finds his own weakness.* He never becomes convinced of the surge and flow of the infinite resources and the riches of His Grace until he stands unclothed in his own poverty and nakedness. It is only as we decrease that He will increase. Recognition of God's fullness is predicated on recognition of our emptiness.

Faith comes from God and from God alone. "Faith *cometh.*" "Faith COMETH"! "FAITH COMETH!" If it comes from within, it is only because God is there. You can search the heights and explore the depths, but you will never find the origin of faith any other place than in God Himself.

God gives it!

God imparts it!

When faith comes, man ceases from his labors!

There is no sense in struggling to produce faith by yourself, when it can only be produced by God!

Faith—GOD'S FAITH—even if it's only as big as a grain of mustard seed—is sufficient for any need and more than enough for any emergency.

But how does faith come? The inspired Word tells us that "Faith cometh by hearing." In what I am now going to say and in what you are now going to read, I pray the Holy Spirit will give you eyes that can see and ears that can hear. Ordinarily we have taken this scripture to mean that faith will come to us if we listen to sermons.

Ears To Hear

When Jesus walked the shores of Galilee and preached the Word of God, people did not hear. That nearly broke the heart of my Lord. He said many things they could not hear. When Jesus spoke, there were other ears necessary than the two which are fastened on either side of the head. He spoke to them by the seaside, but they could not hear. He talked to them in the streets and in the synagogue, but *they could not hear.*

The religious leaders of the day, well versed in the law, and probably good keepers of the law, came up to Him and tried to trap Him with Scripture. The Master knew that the "letter killeth," and that it was only the Holy Spirit which would make alive. He knew the danger of isolating texts and building upon erroneous interpretations religious edifices in which unyielded and selfish souls might dwell.

It was the same old story repeated over and over again. The people dwelt in the realm of the natural and material, while the heart of Jesus burned with the flaming knowledge that God is a Spirit and "they that worship him must worship him in spirit and in truth" (John 4:24). They were unable to get out of the lower material and natural realm into the spiritual realm, where the voice of the Lord could be heard, and where the real meaning of the Spirit could be unfolded and understood.

The Word

"Faith cometh by hearing, and hearing by the Word of God" (Romans 10:17). Now John the beloved tells us the Word is the Logos and that it was made flesh and dwelt among us. In plain language, it was the Word of God Himself—the voice of God—the still, small voice that appealed not to the intellect, but to the spiritual nature, which would then yield to the voice of God and make the natural and material subject to the spiritual.

How we have turned things around! If we cannot understand something, we want to throw it out. If reason cannot grapple with it, we do not want to receive it as the revelation of God.

In the Garden of Eden, man walked and talked with God. God heard the voice of His creation, man; but I am wondering to what extent man really heard the voice of God. The Creator said, "In the day that ye eat thereof, ye shall die." Then the devil with all his subtlety and malice told man, "Ye shall not surely die.... Ye shall be as gods." Man in his first, flagrant act of disobedience, not only disobeyed God's words but began to figure out, by the "wisdom" of man, how it would be if he disobeyed God. His very actions were a mixture of soulish and spiritual activity. He would know the difference between good and evil! He would partake of the forbidden fruit.

Though he heard the letter of the Word, could it be that he did not perceive the essence of the Spirit of the Word? Why do we not realize that it is not natural understanding of the printed word that we need, but an inward illumination which will make that Word *blaze and burn within the confines of the soul!* This is what will transform us into spiritual men full of God's faith.

Where Is God?

God does not appeal to the mind. He will not bow before the throne of man's reason. He will not subject Himself to the little materialistic things with which we play. His thoughts are not our thoughts. If we would commune with God, we must get into the mainstream of where God is and into the spiritual place in which He manifests Himself and His power.

This was the blazing, burning message of Paul in his Epistle to the Corinthians, in the second chapter! "Now we have received, not the spirit of the world but the spirit which is of God; that we might know the things that are freely given to us of God; which things also we speak, not in the words which man's wisdom teacheth, but which the Holy Spirit teacheth ... but the natural man receiveth not the things of God: for they are foolishness unto him: neither can he know them, because they are spiritually discerned. But he that is spiritual judgeth all things" (2 Corinthians 2:12-15). Let us examine God's faith that changes the destinies of nations.

CHAPTER 5

THE GIFT OF FAITH

A nd Jesus answering saith unto them, Have faith in God. For verily I say unto you, That whosoever shall say unto this mountain, Be thou removed, and be thou cast into the sea; and shall not doubt in his heart, but shall believe that those things which he saith shall come to pass; he shall have whatsoever he saith" (Mark 11:22-23).

I cannot say it often enough, that what you *say* is important. Jesus said, "For verily I say unto you, That whosoever shall *say* . . ." Jesus *said* to the man with the withered hand, "Stretch forth thine hand" (Matthew 12:13). Jesus *said* to the wind and waves, "Peace, be still" (Mark 4:39).

Jesus said to the leper, "I will: be thou clean" (Luke 5:12). Jesus said to Lazarus, "Come forth" (John 11:43).

59

When we declare the Word of the Lord as the word of our testimony, miracles, signs and wonders have to follow.

We are going beyond what people generally think of as faith in this explanation.

Much of what has been expressed as faith is not faith at all. This is not true in every case, but in most cases it will apply.

Mark 11:22 says, "Have faith in God." It could be rendered just as accurately, "Have the faith of God"—it is so translated in the marginal reference.

As I told you, we are now going beyond the surface of faith. We are going beyond presumption (which is not faith at all). We are also passing beyond unbelief, which is not faith either, by its very definition.

Jesus said, "Verily I say unto you, that whosoever shall say unto this mountain, Be thou removed, and be thou cast into the sea; and shall not doubt in his heart, but shall believe that those things which he saith shall come to pass; he shall have whatsoever he saith" (Mark 11:23).

We haven't even begun to see what God wants to do for us. One of the biggest struggles within the Church of Jesus Christ is the struggle to receive faith.

I see this struggle on every level. I see it as people of God get in what they call "healing lines" for prayer. Perhaps you have tried to "get" faith by repeating to yourself over and over, "I believe, I believe. By faith I've got it." And you didn't "get it."

If we are honest with ourselves and with God, we have to confess that most of our spiritual antiques have built more unbelief than faith in God.

This book has been written with a single purpose: that God will replace your life with His life, so that by the grace of God you will never again be the same.

It is the will of God that all the struggling of your soul will cease. God's perfect will is deliverance from spiritual frustration.

The devil has a unique way of tantalizing God's people. You know what I'm referring to. He'll hold just out of your reach the things that you need. When you get a little closer, he moves it away; a little closer, he moves it again. You keep struggling, grasping, trying to get it. Consequently, your whole spiritual life is in a constant state of turmoil.

"There remaineth therefore a rest to the people of God" (Hebrews 4:9). "For he [the person] that is entered into his [God's] rest, he also hath ceased from his own works, as God did from his" (Hebrews 4:10).

Therefore, this moment, we can put to death every struggle. "The natural man receiveth not the things of the Spirit of God ... they are spiritually discerned" (1 Corinthians 2:14).

I hope you have put up your spiritual antennas. We're going to lay the basic foundation which will clear up any misgivings on this subject of faith.

Jesus capsuled faith into an easy-to-understand situation: "Except ye be converted (turn) and become as little children, ye shall not enter into the kingdom of heaven" (Matthew 18:3).

"Except ye become as little children." God didn't complicate Himself. Where would Chris Panos be if God had complicated Himself! I don't know. But this I do know, that our God wants us "to comprehend (know, understand) with all saints what is the breadth, and length, and depth, and height; And to know the love of Christ, which passeth knowledge, that ye might be filled with all the fulness of God" (Ephesians 3:18-19).

The Bible promises, "The eyes of your understanding being enlightened; that you may know the hope of his calling, and what the riches of the glory of his inheritance in the saints" (Ephesians 1:18).

We are going to start in the very simple place where it all begins. I know I am going to shock some people with this statement. I am going to try to help you understand how I don't have a corner on the truth.

I am writing to you what I have learned. Faith is not a product of man's mind. Now I know all about a positive attitude and positive thinking. I know all about Dr. Norman Vincent Peale, and I appreciate him, a fine minister of the Gospel, but we are not talking about the power of positive thinking. It's a sad state of affairs that during the last fifteen years, the Church has gotten the theology of Dr. Peale and the resurrection power of Jesus Christ a little mixed up.

We're not talking about the power of positive thinking. There's not a negative bone in my body. I'm a positive thinker. But it takes more than positive thinking to heal polio!

In this last hour before Jesus comes, the Church (the spotless, pure Bride of Jesus Christ) is coming into the place where the fulness of God indwells our being and instills His power into us.

We're going to bypass the natural (including positive thinking with the natural mind) and enter as overcomers into the spiritual. "For though we walk in the flesh, we do not war after the flesh: (For the weapons of our warfare are not carnal [of the flesh], but mighty through God to the pulling down of strongholds;) Casting down imaginations, and every high thing that exalteth itself against the knowledge of God, and bringeth into captivity every thought to the obedience of Christ; And having a readiness to revenge all disobedience, when your obedience is fulfilled" (2 Corinthians 10:3-6).

That's why I have a message to those who get into a healing line repeating, "I believe, I believe."

You've asked me, "Brother Panos, how does a person believe?"

I'll answer this way: at the beginning, when you come to Jesus Christ, how are you saved? Are you saved by an act of faith?

Someone said, "Every man is given a measure of faith." I challenge that statement. Every man is *not* given a measure of faith. That statement from Romans 12:3 is lifted out of context.

Do you know to whom God gives a measure of faith?

"I beseech you therefore, brethren, by the mercies of God, that ye present your bodies a living sacrifice, holy, acceptable unto God, which is your reasonable service.... according as God hath dealt to every man the measure of faith" (Romans 12:1,3).

Don't tell me that drunkard in the honky-tonk downtown has faith. You may *think* he has—if you don't understand what faith is.

Don't tell me that prostitute in the hotel in your city

has faith. She might be considered to have faith, if you don't understand what faith is. But when you understand that faith is a spiritual quality and not a natural quality, then you are able to put the matter in perspective.

It's true that every man can believe, if you call positive thinking belief. Each person has the power of positive thinking. Through positive natural thinking a man can change his life from one of insecurity, darkness and failure to the point where he experiences a measure of success. But there is a difference between that experience of positive thinking and the experience of *faith*, like the difference between night and day.

When a baby is born, its first function is to demonstrate its will. God made us in His image. The way He made us like gods was to give us authority, to give us our own will, and the power to rule over that will. That's the only primary power we have. We can chose to obey God, or to disobey Him.

That's the great moral of the story of Adam and Eve. Adam didn't *have* to love or obey God. Neither did Eve. But God so loved Adam and Eve that He desired to be with them. In the beginning, God would come to Adam and sup with him. Adam would worship God out of a willing heart. He was giving God that which was rightfully His. He would keep His Word, and he would obey Him willingly.

But Adam took his will and used it directly to disobey God. Adam and Eve disobeyed the "thus saith the Lord" in the simple test God had provided for them.

When they disobeyed, they were cast out of the family of God. They were ostracized. And from that day till now there has been only one purpose with God: to bring His creation back into the right relationship with God that Adam enjoyed before the fall.

All through the Old Testament, through the New Testament, by the Blood of the Paschal Lamb, through the Blood of Jesus Christ, there has been only one purpose in God's mind: restoration.

He searched for a plan to bring the fallen adamic race back to Himself.

In your own mind and by your own ability, you cannot have faith to appropriate the atoning work of Jesus Christ. You don't have this strength in yourself.

There is only one power given to man: the power to rule and reign over his own will. And what is the work of the Holy Spirit? To cause that will to yield itself *willingly* to God so He can work and move in our beings. He moves to turn over the fallow ground inside our beings.

God does this through the conviction of preaching, through the moving of the Holy Spirit, and through the demonstration of the power of God.

As the Holy Spirit begins to move in our hearts, we begin to feel it. Then a song wells from deep within,

> All that I am
> All that I have
> All I shall ever be
> Cannot repay the love-debt
> I owe.
> I surrender to Thee.

When we surrender, then God begins to move upon our hearts. When we preach salvation and the Spirit of

God comes into a service, God moves upon the hearts of the people.

You can say yes to the Holy Spirit, or you can say no. You cannot save yourself, but the Holy Spirit can.

The initial power to believe that Jesus Christ is the Son of God is a gift of God. You surrender your heart and faith, that super-natural power God gives so that you can accept the new life, comes through Jesus Christ and His finished work on Calvary.

When you came to the altar of God, and surrendered yourself to the moving of the Holy Spirit, you said yes to God. The Bible declares that, "as many as received him [as many as yielded to Him] to them GAVE HE POWER to become the sons of God, even to them that believe on His Name" (John 1:12).

It is "By grace are ye saved through faith, and that not of yourselves; it is the gift of God: Not of works, lest any man should boast" (Ephesians 2:8-9). You are given faith so that you can be saved by grace at the moment you surrender.

The moment you surrender to God,

The instant that you surrender to the wooing of the Spirit of God,

At the very moment you make a surrender of yourself—God takes over.

He infuses us with His power and with His supernatural glory, and we are saved. "Whosoever shall call on the name of the Lord shall be saved" (Acts 2:21).

I pray that God may open your spiritual eyes to the depth of this truth.

Every move Jesus made was for a divine purpose. The Bible declares that when Jesus got to the fig tree,

66

he found nothing but leaves, "for the time of figs was not yet" (Mark 11:14).

Did Jesus know it wasn't yet time for figs? Since He *did* know, He must have had a lesson He wanted to teach His disciples. I believe it was simply, "Have the faith of God."

The most important truth presented here is: man has nothing and is nothing in himself. "A man can receive nothing, except it be given him from Heaven" (John 3:27).

You can memorize the whole Bible and yet not get faith.

Many who believe that Jesus is the very Christ are going to hell! You ask how? I tell you Jesus will not be responsible for their fate. They will be responsible for their fate. Jesus has never, and will never, send any person to hell! Jesus only *allows* the final choice of every person to remain as that one *chose*. Jesus *will not* take anyone to heaven against his will. Lord Jesus has paid the price on Calvary for your *love*. He has bought your *peace* with the tortures of the Cross. He purchased your right to *joy* with His own blood. But you have to accept the gift He purchased.

You didn't come to the altar repeating over and over, "I love people." No! You came to the Cross, with no love, no joy, no peace. You came simply and surrendered your heart and will to Jesus at the foot of the Cross. Then "the love of God [was] shed abroad in [your] heart by the Holy Ghost which was given to us" (Romans 5:5). In yourself you could never love the unlovely. When you do, it's God's love working through your heart!

What about peace? Did you get peace by reading a book? By becoming a positive thinker? Did you go through a ritual, "I've got peace, I've got peace"?

Most emphatically, NO!

Jesus said, "Peace I leave with you, my peace I give unto you, not as the world giveth, give I unto you. Let not your heart be troubled, neither let it be afraid" (John 15:27).

Peace and fear cannot live together in the same house. When fear leaves, peace can reign.

"And the peace of God, which passeth all understanding, shall keep [guard] your hearts and minds [thoughts] through Christ Jesus" (Philippians 4:7).

And joy. How did you get joy? After you had tried everything in the world, you came to the foot of the Cross. When the presence of Jesus flooded your being, you received joy. Joy unspeakable and full of glory.

Man in himself has nothing except he receive it from above. If you can't work up joy, if you can't work up peace, if you cannot create love, what is it that energizes and keeps the Church of Jesus Christ?

If the "greatest of these is charity [or love]" (1 Corinthians 13:13), and you can't manufacture that, how much less can you manufacture faith? Truly, you must "have the faith of God" (Mark 11:22, margin).

When you understand it's not your love, nor your joy, nor your peace, then there is no struggle.

No longer will you feel like pulling your hair, or wondering in desperation, "Why can't I believe!" You won't have to fear that God doesn't hear your prayer. When you realize that it's not you who has to do these things, then the struggle is over!

It's not you, because "I am crucified with Christ: nevertheless I live; yet not I, but Christ liveth in me: and the life which I now live in the flesh I live *by the faith of the Son of God*" (Galatians 2:20). I live by the faith that Jesus has!

It's not Chris Panos with his weak, feeble mentality and ability. It's not Chris Panos with all his sinful nature. "For I am crucified with Christ."

Christ lives in me!

Christ lives *in* me!

Christ's *love* lives in me!

Christ's *peace* lives in me!

Christ's *joy* lives in me.

And now Christ's *faith* is in me! Therefore, I cannot fail. I shall therefore arise and take my place in the Kingdom of God.

I shall arise in the strength of the blood-stained banner of Calvary. I shall arise in my Redeemer's faith and say to this mountain, "Be thou removed!"

Thank you, dear Lord, there's no unanswered prayer. There's no conflict. There's no struggle. The power of God is beside every person who dares to have God's faith.

You won't be the same when you realize this: when you were born again, God's faith was placed inside you. You just didn't recognize it. "As many as received him, to them *gave* he power" (John 1:12).

God's faith is already in you to do the good pleasure of God. In every area of your life His faith is in you.

You will no longer live a roller coaster life. It won't be the devil winning the victory one day while you take it the next. "Greater is he that is in you, than he that is in the world" (1 John 4:4).

69

Now that you see this—

There's no defeat.

There's no despondency.

There's no struggle.

We have become victors through Jesus Christ our Lord.

There's not a habit that can bind you.

There's not an evil thought that can possess you.

Glory to God!

I want to give my life anew to God. I want Jesus Christ to forgive me of every sin and failure. I want to make an honest, clean-cut surrender to God through Jesus Christ right now.

If God appeared in a visible form and told you to go down to the corner, and if you didn't hesitate at all, but walked right down to the corner, what would that be? That's right! Obedience.

By the power of the Spirit, Abraham saw God in the night. What did Abraham do? He believed God (and in believing, he *obeyed* God) and it was counted to him as righteousness (Galatians 3:6).

"The Lord appeared unto Abram, and said unto him, I am the Almighty God; walk before me, and be thou perfect" (Genesis 17:1). Is there any sinless, perfect one on this earth? No! Jesus Christ was the only perfect One who is without sin.

Yet God commissioned Abram to walk before Him and to be perfect! What did He mean? God never requires more of anyone than he can fulfill. (The Hebrew word rendered "perfect" means complete, entire, whole.) God was saying, "Grow up Abraham! Be complete in Me!" The word for "Almighty God" in

70

verse 17 is *El Shaddai.* The Lord said, "Let Me be your El Shaddai." *El* is Elohim in all His strength and power. *El* is God the omnipotent, all-powerful Creator of heaven and earth. *El* is the God who *knows* all, and *sees* all, and who *performs* all things for His people.

The other word, *Shaddai,* is beautifully tender. *Shad* is the Hebrew word for a woman's breast.

A little, helpless, newborn baby gets everything it needs from its mother's breast. The little child draws the milk from its mother's breast and, when it does, that milk becomes its strength. It goes into the bones and sinews of its body to nourish the life of the child. It causes the child to live and to grow in strength.

God was saying to Abraham, "I am your All-Sufficient Source of help and strength."

"Abraham, I am your life."

"I, Jehovah God (*El Shaddai*) am your strength. I am your nourishment, Abraham. I am your food, Abraham. Draw your life from Me! Walk before Me and be thou perfect.

"Abraham, you don't have to walk in your own strength. You don't have to depend on your own power and ability. Draw from God, Abraham."

This is a reference to God's power to supply *all* the needs of His people. In this occurrence in Genesis 17:1, it is used to show Abraham that He Who called him out to walk alone before Him could supply all his need.

How marvelously high above our ways are the ways of God. Only *El Shaddai* could be a "nursing father"! It is His desire to care for each of His children with

71

wisdom and love far surpassing anything we could ever think or imagine; yet He wants us in our weakness as we face great difficulties to cry out to Him. What will your faith subdue today?

CHAPTER 6

FAITH QUENCHES THE VIOLENCE OF FIRE

W ho through faith subdued kingdoms, wrought righteousness, obtained promises, stopped the mouths of lions, Quenched the violence of fire, escaped the edge of the sword, out of weakness were made strong, waxed valiant in fight, turned to flight the armies of the aliens" (Hebrews 11:33,34).

"By faith they passed through the Red Sea as by the dry land: which the Egyptians assaying to do were drowned" (Hebrews 11:29).

Strong men have always failed, always been defeated; only those who have cried out to God in complete total surrender have conquered. Moses, when he began his walk with God, cried out, "Look who I am." But when he finished forty years in the wilderness, he asked, "Who am I?" Moses, who had all the wisdom of Egypt, was unable to cope with the situations that faced him. He was terrified even to speak, even to hold a face–to–face conversation with man, but—praise God—he was able to commune with the Holy One of Israel. Weak yet strong, Moses' weakness was God's strength.

Yes, "By faith they passed through the Red Sea." His grace is sufficient, whatever the pathway; His strength in your weakness is perfect. For "my strength is made perfect in weakness" (2 Corinthians 12:9). "The Lord shall fight for you and ye shall hold your peace" (Exodus 14:14).

"The LORD said unto Moses, Wherefore criest thou unto me?" (Exodus 14:15). Speak now and tell them to "go forward." Moses was faced with death. He feared the Egyptians. He was afraid of all the horses and chariots of Pharoah, of Pharoah's horsemen and his army. Pharoah drew near and the children of Israel lifted up their eyes, saw the Egyptians, and were afraid, crying out to Moses—accusing him. Moses, faced with these extreme circumstances, cried out to God for a miracle. He was desperately and totally relying on God. This type of attitude always receives God's help and strength. This attitude always triumphs.

I remember an extreme circumstance: I was on an airplane that was filled with Communists. I had a German overcoat on and it was filled with Gospels. It was so full that I didn't dare take it off. I knew if I folded it and laid it above on the rack it was very possible that it would fall. So I just kept it on. The airline had no luxury racks or comfortable seats. It was a war plane converted into a commercial domestic carrier. It seemed as if the enemy was closing in on every side. Three Red Chinese soldiers were heading my way. They did not crack a smile and they looked very hard at me (as though they were staring daggers at me). Believe me, I was very consecrated! I was made strong; I was weak, yet strong. In my weakness I was made strong by God. I was totally depending on God to help me. Like Moses I cried out, "Lord, help me!" Then the lightning flashes of God's Spirit took hold of my spirit! And all of a sudden I obeyed the divine flow of love that constrained me to stand and speak "the words of life," as the Spirit of God flashed through my spirit. That love of God, that miracle-working substance called love, leaped over onto those three Red Chinese soldiers—and saturated them from the crowns of their heads to the bottoms of their feet. A smile seemed to ooze out. They cracked a smile from ear to ear. I told them their Red Mao badges were very pretty.

I was impregnated now with the abundant divine love of God. I told of the invisible badge I wore, and that it had all power in heaven and on earth. It was the name of Jesus Christ. The love of God flowed from my spirit to theirs. The divine flowing super-power of God's love transmitted life. I spoke of a Christ who went to Calvary to die for their souls. I told them that the blood of Jesus cleanses us from all unrighteousness. Then in a twinkling of an eye I challenged them to take Christ. They gave me their Mao badges and received my invisible badge, Jesus Christ the Son of God. I was weak, helpless; yet I was also strong and powerful, for God's divine love was flowing in and through me. I was surrounded by the enemy; yet when I cried out to God for a miracle, God answered and made me more than a conqueror in the midst of defeat. My God blew away all obstacles.

Can you see the armies of Pharaoh drawing near? Can you see the Red Sea standing before you, making escape impossible? Moses was completely and totally surrendered to God; therefore God moved and supplied the necessary weapons beyond man's own reasoning. The supernatural was reached, because of Moses' total, consecrated surrender. God moved a strong east wind, and the Lord God caused the sea to roll back and made dry land appear as the waters were divided. And the children of Israel were saved.

Have you surrendered your life to Jesus Christ? If you have not, now is a good time to yield to the tugging of the Holy Spirit. Surrender now and God will cause a miracle to take place in your life. "As many as received him, to them gave he power to become the sons of God" (John 1:12). "My grace is sufficient for thee: for my strength is made perfect in weakness" (2 Corinthians 12:9). "Whosoever shall call upon the name of the Lord shall be saved" (Acts 2:21). Stand still and see the salvation of the Lord. "The grass withereth, the flower fadeth: but the word of our God shall stand for ever" (Isaiah 40:8). Hallelujah!

I am speaking particularly to backsliders. Not only to the confessed backsliders, but to the unconfessed backsliders. There are a lot of people trying to ride along on the experiences and glories of yesterday, and yet in their hearts they are yearning for an up-to-date experience with God. The Lord has departed from Israel, and instead of the sunshine of His presence there has been a shadow of fear and doubt upon them. If this is your problem, there is only one answer. His name is Jesus.

Don't live in the past! Don't you see? We must be alive! Christ must be alive! He *is* alive! Christians can't afford to rest on past experiences. Turn away from the world now—surrender to the cross now—receive His healing power now! His power is past understanding, His grace is sufficient to meet your need. If you are willing, He is willing—turn now, confess your sins to Jesus Christ. Surrender right now! Ask to be made right with Him. If you have never received Him, ask Him to come into your heart. Receive Him, and be saved.

Yes, they "quenched the violence of fire," overcame every circumstance, "escaped the edge of the sword, out of weakness were made strong" (Hebrews 11:34). They overcame every circumstance. They were sanctified.

What does sanctification mean?

That means to become set apart!

That means to become a peculiar vessel!

That means to become separated from the world!

That means to have those pecularities that the world cannot help but see which will always accompany one who will walk a separated life unto God!

"Love not the world, neither the things that are in the world. If any man love the world, the love of the Father is not in him" (1 John 2:15).

The reason for that is, that when the Lord really saves us—

He does not save us on the outside!

He saves us on the inside!

The Lord does not change a man's life!

He changes a man's heart; and because his heart is changed, his life as a natural man changes also.

You cannot draw bitter water and sweet water out of the same fountain at the same time; and when the heart is cleansed, then out of the heart proceed the things that make the man. When our heart is cleansed, we are going to give to the world streams of living waters. When we are saved, we have a different life, a transformed way of thinking. "And be not conformed to this world: but be ye transformed by the renewing of your mind, that ye may prove what is that good and acceptable, and perfect, will of God (Romans 12:2). A different method of living will be our testimony. So we are sanctified as we surrender to His Lordship. Hallelujah! Out of weakness we are made strong.

Can you see David, the shepherd boy? God can make a king out of a shepherd boy as long as he will keep the shepherd boy spirit!

Can you see David standing in the midst of the children of Israel confused and afraid? No, you see Goliath of Gath defying the whole army of Israel crying, "Give me a man that we may fight together."

David had had two previous experiences, for in the strength of the Lord he had slain the lion and killed the bear. His was a surrendered life—the life of a sweet singer of Israel, singing and praising God, who became bold as a lion. He was a mere stripling, a ruddy youth, but God could use him. Out of weakness they were made strong; they *waxed* (changed) valiant in fight. Yes, David was transformed from a stripling youth to a daring, bold lion risking his life for the sake of the Living God. My friends, he was weak yet strong! Praise the Lord! That's our position when we stay low. Yes, the way up is down, seeking God's face. Being broken constantly before Him, never leaving the presence of the Living God!

David could go forward because he had made up his

mind to go all the way with God, and after he laid aside the armor of Saul and counted it useless to himself, he still reverenced his elders and laid it aside respectfully. That armor is a symbol to me of God's weapons compared to the armor of the world. "For the weapons of our warfare are not carnal but mighty through God to the pulling down of strongholds" (2 Corinthians 10:4). We cannot fight the world with swords.

Or with worldly spears!

Or with worldly guns!

Or with worldly artillery!

For as God was in Christ reconciling the world to Him, so Christ is in us carrying on the work of reconciliation.

The most potent thing in the world is *love*—yes, the most potent things that Christ used were seemingly the weakest things!

And the weakest things were the strongest. "A soft answer turneth away wrath" (Proverbs 15:1). "Vengeance is mine, I will repay, saith the Lord" (Romans 12:19). If your enemy comes against you and you want to overcome him, don't fight him! Please don't talk about him!

But if he is hungry give him food, and if he is thirsty give him drink.

You say that's weakness; but no, that's strength. My weakness is made perfect in God's strength!

If you want to find the only way, I can tell you in just three words.

Come to Jesus!

Not to a system! Not a plan! But to a person!

79

Not to an idea, but to the Son of the Living God! Come to Jesus!

Turn away from your sins and wickedness. If your soul is thirsty, come to the waters by Samaria's wayside well, where that blessed message fell on a woman's thirsty soul long ago! Remember how Jesus said, "If thou knewest who ... thou wouldest have asked him, and he would have given thee living water" (John 4:10).

Yes, "I am the way, the truth, and the life" (John 14:6); "Come unto me, all ye that labour and are heavy laden, and I will give you rest" (Matthew 11:28).

Come to Jesus! How? Stop right now and say, "Lord Jesus, forgive me of all my sins; I receive you as my Lord and Savior." Yes! "Look and live," cried the prophet! Surrender now, be sanctified, and rededicate your life; cry out to God now. "As many as received him, to them gave he power to become the sons of God" (John 1:12). Out of weakness you will be made strong, and God's faith will quench the violence of fire that so easily besets you.

CHAPTER 7

FAITH THAT MARCHES ALONE

When God desires to shake, or shock, or shape any age or generation to bring about a revival, one significant fact inevitably stands out: He always works through individuals. When Israel was in bondage in Egypt, God sent one man, Moses, with the power and authority to deliver them. When Haman conspired to massacre all the Jews, God sent one woman, Esther, to defeat Haman's evil plan.

The fourth chapter of Judges recounts the twenty-year oppression of Israel by Sisera, the captain of the hosts of the Canaanites. All the combined armies of Israel had not been able to defeat Sisera, not even once in those twenty terrible years. When Israel cried out to God for help, He raised up one woman, Deborah the prophetess. That one woman, under God, kindled such a flame that it swept across the armies of Sisera like a prairie fire, utterly destroying them. Then, when Sisera fled for his life, it was another woman—a solitary woman, named Jael—who completed the destruction of this mighty captain, formerly the conqueror of kings.

I am sure you are thinking, as I am, of all the other times God has used individuals to deliver nations: Elijah, Elisha, Daniel, and all those others whose names we revere today.

Rigidly regimented religious organizations, bound by the restrictive trappings of creeds and traditions, super-systematized into powerless ceremonialism, have become too ponderous to be used in the lightning-like thrusts of instant revival by which God stirs nations.

There comes a time, like right now, when the need cannot wait any longer. The crisis has simmered until it has reached the boiling point, and it has to be met NOW. It cannot wait for boards and committees to pass on ways to meet it, for by that time, the opportunity may well have been lost forever.

Computerized religion, with its ponderous platitudes, has very nearly destroyed its effectiveness by reducing its members to mere visionless, meaningless ciphers of a total mass. Individual initiative has been virtually destroyed, and people who might have risen to the heights of noble Christian action are dragged down to the depths of do-nothing despondency. How can there be much fire in the pew when there is so little fire in the pulpit? How can the people be expected to have a burning, driving vision, when the eyes of their leaders are obscured by the cataracts of compromise?

Never, NEVER—in all the history of the Church—has God ever been able to revive a religious organization or denomination as a whole. Instead, He has had to use individuals. He has called out one here and one there, filled them with His power, set them ablaze with His divine purposes, implanted His principles within them, and used them to bring about great revivals.

The individuals whom He has used have always been those who refused to be cut down to fit the limited pattern of standardized religion. They refused to wear the dark glasses of doubt. They refused to parrot the meaningless, trite phrases of uninspired theology. They refused to surrender their God-given initiative. When they were called fanatics, they accepted that title as a mark of distinction. They were persecuted, but they persevered.

Sometimes these God-called individuals suffered disgrace, but still their flaming witness ignited a torch which dispelled the darkness and pointed the way to God. They were often driven to the caves, but just as often they shouted from the mountain tops. Many of them were crucified, but still they conquered. They moved mountains, wrought righteousness, and subdued kingdoms. They quenched the violence of fire, stopped the mouths of lions, and rose to such heights of selfless heroism that the Bible, after citing their exploits, says, "Of whom the world was not worthy" (Hebrews 11:38).

It was not a crowd that produced the majestic miracles on Mt. Carmel; it was an individual, Elijah, a hero who dared to march alone. It was not a crowd that produced the miracle of the divided Red Sea; it was an individual, Moses, a hero who dared to march alone. It was not an army that leveled the blaspheming Goliath in the dust of defeat; it was a young shepherd boy, David. He too dared to march alone. It was not a committee that wrote the Pauline Epistles—those "shady green pastures" of spiritual revelation where we feast upon the riches of God's grace—it was a tentmaker, Paul. His consecration survived one crisis after another, and even when all those which were in Asia turned away from him, he marched on, alone.

It was an individual, Philip, who brought about the sweeping revival in the city of Samaria—a revival so great that demons were cast out, the lame walked, the people were healed of palsy, and the whole city reverberated with shouts of joy.

When Jesus came, bringing the message of salvation and deliverance, He did not entrust that message to the politically powerful Pharisees, or to the intellectual Sadducees. Instead, Jesus went down to the seashore and hand-picked individuals like Peter, James, John, and Andrew, to become His disciples. And straightaway, these rugged individuals left their nets and marched into the pages of history, eternally immortalized as deliverers.

Rome ruled the world when Jesus appeared on the scene, but Jesus didn't enlist Rome's iron legions to proclaim His message and enforce His dominion. Instead, He went to the people and sought out individuals—a fisherman here, a tax collector there, a physician somewhere else. All of these were humble people, bound in by oppressing, limiting circumstances. But when they heard and answered the call of Jesus, something phenomenal happened to them—and they became heroes who dared to march alone.

Today, in the religious world, it is the common practice to play along with the majority, to attempt to know the right people, and never, never, become involved with such "fanatical" beliefs as healing by faith, or the baptism of the Holy Spirit. People are expected to meekly accept uninspired, insipid, watered-down, theological versions of the tremendous sin-conquering, disease-destroying, death-defying themes of Holy Writ. This is the common practice, but it is all wrong. God is looking for individuals who want to hear from heaven. He is looking for individuals who have courage to swim against the tide—heroes who will dare to march alone.

God is not going to reactivate or re-energize the ponderous, creaking apparatus of self-satisfied religious organizations. The needs of the world will not wait for this slumbering leviathan to be aroused. A thousand million heathen are surging up from the slave pits of oppression, and they are cutting squarely across the political consciousness of the world. Listen to the sullen whispers of yesterday's revolution! After centuries of injustice, the heathen are now clamoring for restitution, and their very numbers, combined with their determination, make them a force to be reckoned with. They are drawn taut, like an arrow in the bow of fate, aimed directly at the heart of tomorrow. Either these lost millions will be won to Christ, which will establish their feet on the road to peace, or they will sweep across the world like a dark scythe, reaping a harvest of horror.

Uninspired religion has had centuries to reach and win these masses, but the old methods and the comparatively few missionaries that they deigned to send and support, have not sufficed—and now the time of reckoning has arrived. Our time is measured in days and

85

hours. Every hour that action is delayed is like a treasure lost forever. Every day spent in procrastination brings us inexorably nearer to our Armageddon.

The trumpet of God is sounding out the call to battle. He is looking for individuals just like you—individuals He can call His own—for if He really has an individual wholly dedicated to Him, then that person will have His vision. My friend, God wants you, yourself. He wants to place His faith in your soul, His power in your life, His love in your heart, and the sickle of His Word in your hand. Then He wants to send you out to reap the ripened harvest of the world. Many may try to discourage you, even preachers may try to dissuade you, and Satan may try to prevent you, but heed them not. Listen only to the call of God: "Go ye into all the world, and preach the gospel to every creature" (Mark 16:15). GO by means of your prayers. GO by means of your personal witness. GO by means of your sacrifices. GO by means of your support of radio and television ministries. GO by means of the printed page. GO by means of everything at your command.

In the confused welter of today's religious world, it is sometimes hard to find Jesus, but if you will close your eyes to everything else, you will see Him. And when you see Him, you will find that His face is turned away from the sham and hypocrisy of superficial, dead religion; you will find Jesus facing and moving toward the wide sweeps of earth where lost and forgotten multitudes are fearfully watching the gathering storm.

The message of the Kingdom was never meant to be contained behind church walls; it was meant to inflame the world. And God never intended for you to be shut off from the needs of mankind; He meant for you to be a witness with power, with faith.

God is calling you, my Christian friend. He is asking you to take the unpopular way. He is asking you to step out from among the crowd and dare to be different. If you are willing to enlist wholeheartedly in His service—if you are willing to be a hero who dares to march alone—He will put in your heart the faith of Abraham, the courage of Elijah, the strength of Samson, the death-defying determination of Paul, and the vision of John the Revelator—and you will experience the very same kind of victory they experienced.

God is searching and finding individuals today who are willing to lay their lives on the altar of service. He is laying His hand on individuals, here, there, and everywhere. A great army is being raised up for the Lord—an army of individuals who are going forth courageously, unafraid, filled with the Spirit—carrying a message of hope and life to those who languish in sin and shame, with certain death awaiting them. AND THESE INDIVIDUALS ARE GOING TO SHAKE THE WORLD.

My friend, I have resolved before God that I am willing to be one of those who dare to march alone. Will you be one of that number—one of those heroes who dare to march alone—one whom God can use in this hour? Don't say, "I'm not a preacher, I'm just a clerk ... I'm just an engineer ... I'm just a secretary ... I'm just an accountant ... I'm just a receptionist ... I'm just a home builder and developer." Paul was a tentmaker! David was a shepherd! Peter was a fisherman! God has always called those who are willing to yield themselves to Him. You don't have to be great in the natural. All you have to do is be willing to yield yourself to Him and let Him use you. He will empower you. He will endue you with "power from on high" and make you a shining light—a living witness—if you will just yield yourself wholly to Him as an individual, and dare to march alone.

CHAPTER 8

FAITH THAT SHAKES THE SOUL

One of my real purposes in publishing this book has been to build fiery faith. We know that all the great and wonderful things God has promised to do for us are released to us by faith. We know those passages, "All things are possible to him that believeth" (Mark 9:23). "Without faith it is impossible to please God" (Hebrews 11:6). "Let him ask in faith, nothing wavering" (James 1:6). And again that the "prayer of faith shall save the sick, and the Lord shall raise him up" (James 5:15).

Yes, we know that it's prayer and praise of faith, not the prayer of many words, or the prayer that takes a lot of time, or the prayer full of energy that avails with God. It is the prayer that is of faith that is our victory. How to have a strong, robust, fiery faith life has been one of the most earnest questions of my Christian life.

And to build this kind of faith life into others has been the deep, burning desire of my spirit.

Now the Bible says, "A faithful man shall abound with blessing" (Proverbs 28:20). What shall happen to the man full of faith? God says, "He shall abound with blessing." This word "abound" literally means to overflow. Blessings from God, the rich blessings that come from heaven, the blessings of the Lord, are the reward of the person full of fiery faith. And why should we not be full of faith, when we are the children of God? We are members of the household of faith. God has given to everyone (who has presented their bodies as a living sacrifice—Romans 12:1-2) a measure of faith.

Paul said in 2 Corinthians 4:13, that we received the spirit of faith, so it is quite natural that we should all be full of faith. Not full of unbelief but full of living, burning, vibrant, power-filled faith.

The Manifested Word In Communist Countries

I remember how God spoke to me in November 1967, "I want you to go to East Germany, Hungary, Czechoslovakia, Poland, and Russia. Make thyself ready and go." Every fiber of my being was electrified with the liquid power spoken by the Holy Ghost! At that time I had very little in my bank account and my wife asked, "Chris, how are you going to go with no money?" It is strange how the word of faith manifests itself through us when we really don't have an answer in the natural. I said, "But my God shall supply all my need" (see Philippians 4:19). She said, "How much do you think you will need?" I said, "One thousand dollars." She said, "Darling, where will you get a thousand dollars?" I said, "God will give it to me." After I said that, I said, "I am going to Austin, Texas to speak at a newly-organized fellowship. Pack my bags and have them ready. I am leaving this weekend."

When I began to speak that night in Austin, Texas, I sensed the warm presence of the Holy Spirit in a great way. After the meeting, a man walked up to me and said, "How much do you need to go to Eastern Europe?" I said, "A thousand dollars." He said, "That's what I thought you were going to say. Let me pray tonight about this." The next morning he came over and gave me a thousand dollars to "go and preach the Gospel."

Praise the Lord! In my raincoat, dressed for Texas weather (which does not get very cold), I left for Washington, D.C. I met Brother Andrew (*God's Smuggler*) there and as we went to his room to pray, he spoke as though God had given him this amazing information in advance; he said that I would win many souls in East Germany and that God was with me. God always confirms His Word that He speaks to His servants. Brother Andrew said, "Chris, you are a pioneer like me. You will reach people that I would never reach." After our sweet fellowship, God led me to take a jet out to Frankfurt, Germany, and visit a Brother and Sister Loffert. They were glad to see me again and she makes the best cheesecake in the world. I spoke in their small fellowship about my plans, and they were all amazed. Yet one by one they came and bestowed gifts upon me. God knew I needed a heavy overcoat, so one man gave me his. Another gave me a scarf. The pastor, Brother Loffert, gave me his sweater and long-johns and I was outfitted right down to heavy socks. Praise the Lord! My faith was under fire yet it was full of fire!

Yes, a faithful man, a man full of fiery faith, shall abound with blessings—shall overflow with blessings. The blessings of having his prayers answered, of having healing and health, of having his needs supplied. Yes, great blessings come to those who are full of faith.

There is one Bible way for your faith to increase, for you to be filled to overflowing faith. That is by the Word of God. Romans 10:17 says, "So then faith cometh by hearing and hearing by the Word of God." That is why I urge you, my friends in Christ, to practice saying God's Word daily. Every time you speak out the promises of God, you are building faith. Whenever your ears hear God's Word spoken, faith, fiery faith, is being produced. That is why I wrote this book—to build your faith. What is our secret? Simply speaking the Words of God.

But you can be your own faith builder! Every time you break the silence that fear would prompt with a bold fiery declaration of "thus saith the Word of God," you are building yourself up, strengthening your faith. Your ears hear your own lips speak God's Word and that is faith's sword, the Word of God.

My faith was under fire in having no finances; but thank God, the Word of God controls circumstances. Suddenly I had enough finances. God opened new and strange doors in Bulgaria, Hungary, Russia, and Poland. It seemed, as I was on my way to Budapest with many Gospels and some New Testaments on the train, that the blessed Holy Spirit had gone before me to make the crooked way straight.

Believe me, my faith was under fire. The devil had zeroed in on Chris Panos. The devil said, "You will be checked through customs and they will find the Gospels and you will be arrested." The very air was pregnant with trouble. As the train neared its destination the guards boarded and checked the passengers, looked at many of them and thoroughly checked them. (Believe me it is not like this now; it still is in Red China, but not in Eastern Europe. They have relaxed somewhat.)

The devil was pressing in with all of his forces and speaking his words of defeat in my mind. Then suddenly God spoke, "Son, arise and make ready to depart from the train. Fear not, neither be discouraged but take courage and follow me." Praise the Lord! I felt such a release of faith that I arose zealous, burning with an increased faith full of fire like a torch that could burn through any Iron Curtain wall.

Then God spoke again. Faith cometh by hearing God's Word. "Son, this is the way, walk in this door."

All the people were going through another door about a hundred feet further down. The God of Heaven had imparted fiery faith that swallowed up defeat in victory through His words. I walked through the first doors untouched, unknown, helpless, powerless, yet untouched by the powers of darkness.

After miraculously going through another door (one that was used only by diplomats), I skipped going through customs and having my luggage checked. Outside a taxi waited to take me to my hotel.

It is strange how God speaks the Word of Faith to us; yet it is simple, especially when we are caught off guard and helpless. Then He manifests His Word through our own spirit.

Remember this principle when you are searching in your Bible for a word, and are seeking some sister, brother, pastor, or evangelist to encourage you. Listen to the Holy Living Word—God's voice. The manifested Word is God. Now I don't mean you don't need to read the Word of God. I read ten chapters daily to receive life in order to meet all my daily needs. We must have fellowship with others. But what I want to zero in on is that most Christians never hear the Living Word of Faith! The Word always ran swiftly before me into Russia and Poland, and the Christians in those countries always seemed to know I was coming.

Have Daring Faith

A real key to success is that what we confess or say today, we possess tomorrow—whether it is good or bad, sickness or health, lack or financial prosperity. Did you ever observe that those who are constantly talking about fear are usually quite fearful? If you think it through, you will discover that the ones who constantly talk about lack, experience lack as their master. Yes, it is true that our words produce the kind of life we have. The Bible says, "Thou shalt also decree a thing, and it shall be established unto thee" (Job 22:28). It shall become a part of your life. Yes, it is true that what you continually say is what you receive. I trust you will allow this truth from the Bible to sink deep into your life. When you decree a thing, you will have that thing. God says that when you or I decree a thing, it shall be established unto us.

When you state a thing, you actually speak it into your life. If you speak want, you will have want as your master. But if you decree that God's supply is yours, then you will have His supply. If you decree weakness, then you will have weakness. But if you decree the fact that the Lord is the strength of your life, then you will know His strength. If you decree God's supply of courage, as I did when I got off the train in Budapest and skipped customs, then you will be courageous, rather than fearful. You will be successful and walk through the valley of the shadow of death and say like David, "I will fear no evil." That's faith under fire.

Yes, God says, "Thou shalt decree a thing and it shall be established unto thee." Jesus said the same thing in Mark 11, when He declared, "Whosoever shall say, and not doubt in his heart, but shall believe those things which he saith shall come to pass, he shall have whatsoever he saith." Whatever you say, or decree, can become a reality in your life, if you continually, daily, *say* what you decree until you get it. The words that we speak germinate the presence of faith around us and produce what we say—good or bad, positive or negative, success or failure. If you don't understand this, then you need to read Chapters 1 and 2 again.

Please don't forget this fact: the devil hears our testimony too. The Bible says we overcome the devil by the Word of God in our testimony. But if we have a testimony that lacks the Word of God in it, then the devil will rout us. And if our testimony is not in perfect harmony with God's Word, then the devil will take advantage of us.

Learn to talk about and use God's Word. Talk about God's goodness to you and your fellow Christians. Fill your lips with praise for answers to prayers that you have asked, and as you do so, your faith will grow by leaps and bounds. If you talk about your trials and your difficulties and your lack of money, your faith will shrivel; it will lose its power in your life.

The Bible says in Hebrews 10:23, "Let us hold fast our confession of faith without wavering; (for he is faithful that promised;)" Our part in this life of faith is to hold fast our confession; you do that by saying over and over continually what God says until the petitions you asked for come to pass. God's part is to faithfully fulfill His Word to us, and I promise you He will.

Now the hardest battles in which you will ever be engaged will be along this line. But the greatest battles I have won have been those when everything cried out "impossible!" But impossibilities become realities when we dare to hold fast our confession of God's Word.

First the problem; next the promise; finally the fulfillment of that promise. But in your problem three things can happen: one, you can die there—physically and spiritually; second, you can prolong your stay there like the children of Israel did for forty years in the wilderness; or third, you can stand on the naked Word of God and confess it day and night and never give in to the adversary until you possess what you confess.

Keep up your solid front. God is for you and you cannot be conquered. I promise you that then you will walk in the land of milk and honey and all your petitions will flow your way. You will receive fulfillment. You will see the manifestation of the promise.

The reason some of you are so defeated is that you are living your problem. You are living in the wilderness and you have talked the language of doubt and unbelief. You cannot do that without suffering the consequences. You talk failure and you will fail. But I challenge you to begin to make a bold, confident confession. Dare to be powerful by the words you speak. Be filled with the zeal of God. Tackle and storm through every difficulty by the power of His Words— having daring, rugged, persistent, and fiery faith, the kind of faith that burns with a passion, that wins every time. (Your life is changing even now—something really good is heading your way—you will never be the same again.) Be bold in your faith. Jesus will reward your bold, undenying faith.

The men and the women God uses must pay a price of self-denial, dedication, and hard work to see results produced. It never comes by accident; it is not luck that blessings come our way. God rewards diligent, fiery faith; He rewards hard work and persistent determination to succeed for His glory. We must always acknowledge that God alone makes us sufficient. "Not that we are sufficient of ourselves to think anything of ourselves; but our sufficiency is of God; Who also has made us able ministers of the new testament" (2 Corinthians 3:5-6).

CHAPTER 9

THE TRIUMPH OF FAITH

Second Corinthians 2:14 says, "Now thanks be unto God, which always causeth us to triumph in Christ."

By reading the newspapers today we see what an utter failure man is in this world. Constantly we hear and read negative comments. People face utter defeat in every direction. The world is dying.

The world is yearning for someone to take over all its problems. Satan is getting everybody used to the thought of having one government, one bank, and one church. He's preparing people to yearn and wish and look for a superman who will deliver mankind. But that superman won't really bring peace. He'll bring total destruction.

Our statesmen meet and legislate, appointing committees to investigate causes and remedies. The best minds from all over the world gather together and after much deliberation and debate reach their conclusions, yet the world remains in defeat and uncertainty.

Church leaders are in constant turmoil, a turmoil caused by the fact that many do not really know the Lord they profess to serve. How pitifully weak is the wisdom of this world as it faces the crisis of its life, with history revealing a long record of defeats and failures!

Jesus is the answer.

Natural man is limited—but thanks be to God, there is a place of no defeat. Faith knows no limitations!

There is a place where men can stand and be *more than conquerors.* In the midst of defeat and failure, the Apostle Paul strikes a clear note of victory and gives us the text of this discourse on the triumph of faith: "Now thanks be unto God, which always causeth us to triumph in Christ, and maketh manifest the savour of his knowledge by us in every place" (2 Corinthians 2:14).

What a statement!

God always causeth us to triumph!

Not an occasional victory!

Not a few victories!

But in Christ, God *always* causeth *us to triumph!*

Faith brings the reality of victory in the midst of any and all circumstances! Paul and Silas in the Philippian jail, bound by fetters and with their backs bleeding, sang victorious praises that blew open every door of the prison, loosed every captive, and prepared the way for a manifestation of God the Holy Ghost which brought their jailer to his knees. Seeing the miracle-working power of God, the jailer was saved and baptized. Many are being imprisoned for the Gospel's sake in this twentieth century.

The Man In "Red China"

I remember an old white-haired man in what I will call Red China. He was a beautiful man, dignified and well dressed. His name I cannot tell you, but I can tell you his story. This man was just released from prison because he refused to stop winning souls. The secret police had told him that if he would not preach about salvation and the second coming of Jesus Christ they would not bother him. He refused to stop even if it meant a prison term. I remember how his brothers in Christ asked him, "Why don't you just retire now and let the younger saints win souls? Do as they say; you have paid a great price already. You have been in prison dozens of times for the sake of the Gospel. We love you and don't want you to suffer any more." The glory of God, the triumphant faith of the Living God, seemed to permeate the atmosphere around this man. As he stood in silence, it seemed that a light shone around his whole body. Then he said joyfully, "Brothers and sisters, you see I count it a privilege to suffer just a little for the sake of the Gospel. I am not only willing to be beaten, but I am willing to die for the sake of the Gospel." As we looked him over, we could not fail to see his right and left hands that had been tortured, as the Communists had pulled off all his nails, one after the other. They pulled them off one at a time, slowly, so that the pain might be intensified. And when he turned, I saw that his beautiful face had been marred by a hot branding iron. I can still hear the resounding words of Chou. "I count it a privilege, just a little for the sake of the Gospel. You see I owe a debt to my Master. He died for me; He took my sins; and I must take the Good News to the prisoners in jail, as well as the prisoners on the streets in this country. I must work while it is still day, for night cometh when no man can work." Think about it: this man was willing to be arrested in order to take Jesus Christ to the prisons of his nation. Let me close this testimony with his triumphant faith statement: "I count it a privilege to suffer a little for the sake of the Gospel." "Now thanks be unto God, which always causeth us to triumph in Christ."

The Mysteries of Faith

The natural man cannot believe this good news. He sees only the whipping post, the shackled feet, the iron prison doors, and the darkness of the midnight hour.

The natural man never hears the song of triumph in the midst of apparent defeat, and even if he should hear, he would not understand.

The world and some believers only go to the door of the Philippian jail.

They never see or know anything about the miraculous deliverance—THE TRIUMPHANT FAITH. Faith is the daring of the soul to go further than it can see.

It was this kind of faith that caused Abraham to pursue his triumphant march up to the place of sacrifice and prepare to offer up his only son, believing that God would raise him from the dead.

The world and the unbelieving religionist would watch him go up the mountain and return again with his son, Isaac, and their reasoning minds would say, "Well, he changed his mind. Abraham lost his courage—didn't I tell you he would?"

The reasoner always wants to strike a compromise with the forces of evil. But the believer draws from the resources of heaven.

When Israel, a great host of fleeing slaves, stood helpless and despairing beside the Red Sea with the Egyptian army pressing close upon its heels, the Lord spoke to Moses and said, "Speak unto the children of Israel, that they go forward ... and the children of Israel shall go on dry ground through the midst of the sea" (Exodus 14:15,16).

God said, "Stretch out thine hand over the sea and divide it." (What an order!) But Moses had to act on God's Word!

God has always laid upon His leaders the responsibility of delivering His people, and it is necessary for His leaders to believe and follow the Lord's instructions lest the people perish before the enemy. God instructs believers to heal the sick, laying hands upon them, "and they shall recover" every time.

If Thou Wilt Believe

The same God who told Moses to stretch forth his hand speaks today to every believer saying, "stretch forth your hand in My name and lay it on the sick and they shall recover." "Deliver those who are drawn unto death."

The thousands who are reading this book now are being pressed hard by the devil—by sin, sickness, disease, torment, and trouble. Only the Lord can help. Some cry in agony, forgetting that God said, "If thou canst believe, all things are possible to him that believeth" (Mark 9:23).

Will you be like the old Chinese man who was willing to go forward, no matter what the cost? If you are, your pressures will vanish. Arise and go forward! God's faith will cause you to triumph every time, no matter what your problem is. To God it makes no difference whether the problem is a lost son, or a lost mate, or a lost parent, or some other member of the family. God's faith will conquer your problem whether it is in your marriage or outside of it! Whether it's sin, sickness, poverty, or even death itself that's facing you or your loved ones, God's faith is more than able to meet your need.

Take courage and speak the words of life. "Now thanks be unto God, which always causeth us to triumph in Christ!" (2 Corinthians 2:14). Arise and come out of that prison by releasing the triumphant faith words that abide in you. There is no jail big enough to contain you. There are no chains that can bind you. There is no sin, sickness, or financial need that can hold you. "All power is given unto me in heaven and in earth, Go ye therefore, and teach all nations" (Matthew 28:18,19). Be His disciples! Be His Ambassadors! Now thanks be unto God, Who always causes us to triumph again and again and again through every circumstance!

The Triumphant Faith of Job

It is impossible to leave people exactly as you find them. You will either add something to their lives or take something from their lives. Some people have a contagious good humor. They spread cheer wherever they go. They leave every person they meet just a little better, a little happier than they were before. Whether you realize it or not, whether you want to or not, you contribute, you transmit to every person you meet, either life or death.

Peter said, "Such as I have, give I thee" (Acts 3:6). Paul said, "So, as much as in me is, I am ready to preach the gospel to you that are at Rome" (Romans 1:15). If we give the heathen the Gospel, they will also become like the Christ we give them. Listen to me, your very best days are ahead of you! You can be a powerful witness!

Everything is bound in the will of God. The longer I live with Christ the more I realize we must have a contagious, triumphant faith spirit, the kind we have when prayer has been made and God has entered the scene. How? By sharing your love, you can add to the love of others. By exercising your faith, you can help them to exercise their faith. By having your courage in the face of opposition, you can encourage others to show theirs. This is the contagion of a triumphant spirit.

Job had this kind of faith, and nothing could stifle

the triumphant quality of his faith. It remained constant through all of his material losses, forming a solid foundation through his terrible house of pain, and enabling him to rise above his afflictions. A triumphant faith spirit in touch with God cannot be defeated by sickness or disease of any sort. In the battle that inevitably follows a sudden attack, a triumphant faith spirit will always overcome.

Job was covered with boils from the crown of his head to the soles of his feet. Yet in the midst of this agony, Job's triumphant spirit of faith rose above the corruption of his own decaying body. Through his swollen lips he made a declaration of faith that echoes down the corridors of time and inspires us in this twentieth century.

"For I know that my redeemer liveth, and that he shall stand at the latter day upon the earth: and though after my skin worms destroy this body, yet in my flesh shall I *see God*: Whom I shall see for myself, and mine eyes shall behold, and not another" (Job 19:25-27; italics added). When the Sabeans stole Job's oxen and lightning killed his sheep; when the Chaldeans drove off his camels and a whirlwind killed all of his sons and daughters; it was then that Job fell on his knees and worshipped God (read Job 1:20, 23). There is no way Satan can defeat a triumphant faith spirit like Job's. He had taken away all that Job was and reduced him to be *a governor of an ash heap.* Yet Job's spirit of faith soared on high. Rising above all of the circumstances that had conspired against him, he stood in the mountaintops of faith.

Then there was the triumphant faith spirit of young David, who stood as a dwarf, a midget compared to the giant Goliath, who was nine feet tall. Goliath's armor alone weighed 150 pounds. Was it an unequal contest? It would have been, except for the fact that God had chosen little David to be His champion. He had put within David's heart an optimism, a triumphant faith spirit, that laughed at the formidable odds he faced. Hear the confident voice of David ringing out across the valley: "Then said David to the Philistine, Thou comest to me with a sword, and with a spear, and with a shield; but I come to thee in the name of the Lord of hosts, the God of the armies of Israel, whom thou hast defied. This day will the Lord deliver thee into mine hand . . . that all the earth may know that there is a God in Israel" (1 Samuel 17:45, 46). When the duel was finished, it was Goliath who lay dead in the dust of defeat, and it was David who stood triumphant over his fallen foe.

There was Paul, whose triumphant faith spirit reached out from behind prison walls and dungeon cells to preach the Gospel to uncounted generations.

There was Luther, there was Wesley, there are you and I who spread and are spreading the contagious faith of the Gospel with our lips and lives into the entire world, including Red China. There are no closed doors to the Gospel.

The world today needs Christians who have faith. We need believers who have a triumphant faith spirit and can proclaim victory through the power of God. Each one of us is a sign post, pointing the way either to heaven or to hell. We are living epistles, known and read by everyone we meet.

Everyone living today has an influence that causes others either to lift up or to fall, and that influence is always at work. Let us always keep a contagious, triumphant, spirit of faith. Let us give the world the Good News that Jesus saves. My friends, arise in Christ. Get ready to put into action what you have received. We have won the battle again! Your best days are ahead of you.

CHAPTER 10

FAITH BY THE WORD

Let us read the Word of God and see where the faith of Mary came from.

And in the sixth month the angel Gabriel was sent from God unto a city of Galilee, named Nazareth,

To a virgin espoused to a man whose name was Joseph, of the house of David; and the virgin's name was Mary.

And the angel came in unto her, and said, Hail, thou that art highly favoured, the Lord is with thee: blessed art thou among women.

And when she saw him, she was troubled at his saying, and cast in her mind what manner of salutation this should be.

And the angel said unto her, Fear not, Mary: for thou hast found favour with God.

And, behold, thou shalt conceive in thy womb,

and bring forth a son, and shalt call His name JESUS.

He shall be great, and shall be called the Son of the Highest: and the Lord God shall give unto him *the throne* of his father David:

And he shall reign over the house of Jacob *for ever;* and of *his kingdom* there shall be *no end.*

Then said Mary unto the angel, *How shall this be,* seeing I know not a man?

And the angel answered and said unto her, The Holy Ghost shall *come upon thee,* and the power of the Highest shall *overshadow thee:* therefore also that holy thing which shall be born of thee *shall be called* the Son of God.

And, behold, thy cousin Elisabeth, she hath also conceived a son in her old age: and this is the sixth month with her, who was called barren.

For *with God* nothing shall be impossible.

And Mary said, Behold the handmaid of the Lord; be *it unto me* according to thy word. And the angel departed from her. [Luke 1:26-38; italics added.]

The greatest power in all the world is the expression of the force called faith.

In the birth of our Lord Jesus we have the expression of this force power-packed!

The angel of the Lord came to Mary and promised that she would bear a child conceived not by natural means, but by the Holy Ghost. "The Holy Ghost shall come upon thee." The words spoken to Mary by Gabriel, the angel of the Lord, were enough to give the most spiritual individual reason to stagger! "Therefore also that holy thing which shall be born of thee shall be called the Son of God." Mary looked at the angel and, with full expression of her faith, replied, "Be it unto me according to thy word." She had a total acceptance of the will of God for her life. An inward, mighty, moving, *amen* to Gabriel's "thus saith the Lord" resulted in the fruit of her womb, our precious Lord and Savior Jesus Christ.

Mary demonstrated her faith in God. "With God," the angel declared, "nothing shall be impossible!"

This is the way of faith—Christ's way. Like Mary, we too receive Him into our beings in all His fullness. We receive His quickening life that fills our beings, changes our beings, and puts us in the place where there is always an inward, mighty, moving, God-inspired "amen" to the will of God in our life!

Zacharias and Elisabeth wanted a son. The angel of the Lord appeared to them six months before he appeared to Mary, proclaiming:

Fear not, Zacharias: for thy prayer is heard; and thy wife Elisabeth shall bear thee a son, and thou shalt call his name John.

And thou shalt have joy and gladness; and many shall rejoice at his birth.

For *he shall be great* in the sight of the Lord, and shall drink neither wine nor strong drink; and he shall be filled with the Holy Ghost, even from his mother's womb.

And many of the children of Israel shall he turn to the Lord their God.

And he shall go before him in the spirit and power of Elias, to turn the hearts of the fathers to the children, and the disobedient to the wisdom of the just; to make ready a people prepared for the Lord. [Luke 1:13-17; italics added.]

How destructive and unproductive are the seeds of doubt in a human being! Nothing holds back the will of God for our lives any more than doubt.

"And Zacharias said unto the angel, Whereby shall I know this? for I am an old man, and my wife well stricken in years" (verse 18).

Faith never questions! It accepts the impossible as possible. Faith knows it is not just dealing with natural causes and natural effects, but with the supernatural! With God all things are possible.

And the angel answering said unto him, *I am Gabriel,* that stand in the presence of God; and am sent to speak unto thee, and to shew thee these glad tidings.

And, behold, thou shalt be dumb, and not able to speak, until the day that these things shall be performed, because thou believest not my words, which shall be fulfilled in their season. [Verses 19 and 20; italics added].

Zacharias became dumb and never spoke one word until John the Baptist was born, because he doubted.

There is only one way to all the treasures of God, and that is the way of faith! God has prescribed that the just shall live by faith.

I have often heard it explained that there is "natural" faith and "supernatural" faith, but I cannot agree with this approach. The power of a person's faith is a force greater than any atomic or hydrogen power! Faith

112

has to come from God, and God is supernatural. Daniel Webster said, "Faith is the assent of the mind to divine revelation." What, then, does that man possess who goes through life successfully with his positive mental attitude? Could it be belief? Webster says, "Belief is the assent to anything proposed or declared."

Have you noticed the little rocks on the edge of the mountains, that once were part of the mountain? To look at the rocks and call them "the mountain" would be presumptuous; though a possible part, they are not the mountain itself. So belief is the natural force, the assent to the validity and authority of a matter. But faith is a power that reaches into divine revelation.

When God created man, the Bible says, we were made in the image of God: does this mean our faces, our bodies, our physical features? I don't think so. God put within the creature he created and called "man" a God-like quality: the power of free will! This alone made man like God. Man has the power to choose: he is not forced to do good, to follow his Creator, or to serve his God. But Adam used his power to choose to disobey God, which resulted in our being cursed with the penalty of a sinful nature.

Now how does man come to God? Man does not first come to God; this is the beauty of God's relationship with man: God comes to him, by the wooing, the calling, and the leading of His Spirit. It may be through a particular circumstance or trial in his life. It may be through the reading of God's Word; or through something someone has said which strikes at his heart's door. It may be an evangelistic crusade in a church, or even the reading of this message. God is Spirit. God is everywhere present; He is by your side even now.

No man just comes to God. The Bible says, "We were born, not of blood, nor of the will of the flesh, nor of the will of man, but of God" (John 1:13).

How simple it is: God calls by His Spirit; we sense his call in our beings. Now, we must make a choice: yield to God's voice, His Spirit; or reject God's Son Jesus as our Lord and Savior, reject the only Power available to cleanse our lives from guilt and sin.

The only thing man has to give to God is that which God gave to him when He created him. God waits for us to surrender our will to Him.

You cannot express this power of faith in God in yourself, but you can believe; and if you will believe and yield—that is your part. God will do the rest. The Bible says, "For by grace are ye saved through faith; and that not of yourselves: it is the gift of God: Not of works, lest any man should boast" (Ephesians 2:8-9).

Faith is a gift of God. Man has nothing in himself, unless he receives it from above, like love, joy, and peace. Faith comes only when we make a complete surrender to Him.

Yield to Him now. That is your part: surrender your will. Say yes to God. Then He takes over; He enters your being. With Him comes His faith, enabling you to accept the Divine Revelation. With Him comes the power to live a Christian life. "But as many as received him, to them gave he power to become the sons of God, even to them that believe on his name" (John 1:12).

This can only have meaning for you if Christ becomes the center of your life. Surrender your will to Christ. Give Him the throne room in your life. Crown Him King!

"He shall be great, and shall be called the Son of the Highest: and the Lord God shall give unto him the throne ... and of his kingdom there shall be no end" (Luke 1:32, 33).

Your very best days are ahead of you!

CHAPTER 11

SIX STEPS TO SPIRITUAL POWER THROUGH FAITH

A re the days of miracles over?

When I was last in Israel and in Communist countries, I watched jets streak across the sky, carrying with them their message of destruction.

I have read of the onslaught of Russia against one of her own satellites, Czechoslovakia.

Just recently, I heard that there are seven to eight hundred million Chinese people in the Chinese People's Liberation Army. Armed with Mao Tse Tung thoughts, along with conventional weapons, the Chinese had clashed with the Russians at Sino-Russian borders.

I have often been reminded of the verse, "In the last days perilous times shall come" (2 Timothy 3:1). I'm not an alarmist, but our time is short. I want to plant this truth in your heart: Jesus Christ is coming back very soon. "Behold," said Jesus, "I come quickly." The

Lord is at hand! When Jesus returns, all the blood-washed will be caught up to meet Him in the air. The Church is the Body of Christ, and the Lord will not leave part of His Body behind. But unfortunately for many, not all who call themselves the Church are in reality the Body of Christ.

The Apostate Church is not Christ's Body: only the Church that's washed in the blood will go up in the Rapture. The Lord is coming very soon, and to go with Him, you must be born again.

If I may make a bold statement, I believe that the world will destroy itself in my day. There is coming a battle in which the blood will be up to a horse's bridle, and that battle will only be stopped by the power of the second coming of our Lord. Even so, Lord Jesus, come quickly!

In these last days, many churches have watered down their message to accommodate the mood of the people. In some, the blood of Christ is "a thing of the past." The miracles of Christ are regarded as fiction. And yet, as I minister to the fives and tens and to the thousands and tens of thousands; as I witness to the Jews at the Wailing Wall about Jesus Christ their Messiah; as I see the blind see, the deaf hear, and the lame walk; as I see that the Gospel, the Power of God unto salvation, is being poured out without apology and in all fullness all over the world; and as I see God's prophecies coming to pass one after another; as I see these things, I cannot believe that the day of miracles is over.

I want to go on record saying what God says. God says, "I am the Lord and I change not." "Jesus Christ [is] the same yesterday and today and forever." God doesn't change. He still works miracles. What we need today are more mustard-seed Christians and fewer doubting Thomases! What we need today are mountain-movers, concerned Christians who will take God at His Word and, believing, become His channels for receiving. As the Lord's servant, I promise you that if you can receive by the Holy Spirit what God is unfolding to you in these pages, your whole life and ministry will be revolutionized. God's Word is alive with power! The Bible says:

> But what saith it? the word is nigh thee, even in thy mouth, and in thy heart: that is, the word of faith, which we preach; that if thou shalt confess with thy mouth the Lord Jesus, and shalt believe in thine heart that God hath raised him from the dead, thou shalt be saved. For with the heart man believeth unto righteousness; and with the mouth confession is made unto salvation. (Romans 10:8-10).

There are strange, unusual rumblings in the United States of America. The Word of God in the United States is involved in a spiritual conflict. God's Word has passed through many dangers down through the centuries, but I don't think that it has ever come to what we are facing at this moment. We are going to have to find an answer to the question, "Does the Bible have absolute spiritual authority over us in these days of crisis?"

We are concerned about the social ills of this nation, and not only of this nation but of the entire world. But I wonder if the primary and first principle of business of the Church of Jesus Christ is not the preaching of the Gospel of Jesus Christ. "For what shall it profit a man, if he shall gain the whole world, and lose his own soul?" (Mark 8:36).

I have been all over the world, and I don't say this to build myself up, but I say this so you may understand the authority that is behind the statement I am now going to make. Reporters all over the world have asked questions like these: 1) How do miracles follow your ministry? 2) Does the Bible have absolute spiritual authority for us in these crisis days? Until we answer the second question, there is absolutely no hope of answering the first. Without believing in the absolute spiritual authority of the Word of God, there is no way we can rise up to take all that God has for us in the Holy Scriptures.

Billy Graham said, "I was a normal preacher, until I answered this question." He said, "I went into the woods one day and I asked God why I didn't have power in my preaching." He answered this question in that wooded area where he sought God, and he came out with his Bible under his arm and said, "God, I don't understand everything in this Bible, but one thing I do know is that Your Bible has absolute spiritual authority for me, and I'm not questioning it again as long as I live. I believe the Word of God!"

We have got to believe the Word of God!

We have got to believe the Word of God, because in order to have faith, we have got to fix our faith on something that won't change. Do you know why so many people are disappointed in men? It's because they fix their faith on a certain individual. They fix their faith on the gift that God may have given that individual, not remembering that an individual—like Moses, like David, like Sampson—can fail. Billy Graham can fail; Oral Roberts can fail; Chris Panos can fail. But I want you to know that Jesus Christ never fails.

We need a fixed point for faith—a point that won't change, something that won't say one thing one day and another thing the next. If we fix our faith on the eternal living Word of God, on Jesus Christ, the Son of the Living God, it is impossible for us to be disappointed.

Unless we have something infallible to count on, faith is impossible. We have to have infallibility for faith. If we have infallibility, then we can fix our faith to it, because no wind, no storm, no power will shake it or break it.

There will always be unbelievers. I'm not trying to convince unbelievers. They'll always be there. I'm not worried about the unbelievers—I'm worried about the unbelieving believers!

I am alarmed that in certain quarters some would have the fixed points of our faith—salvation, divine healing, the baptism of the Holy Spirit, the soon coming of Jesus Christ—to go around with every passing wind. They would take the truths of God's impregnable Word and let them turn with every passing new modernistic thought of philosophy or theology or of social economic conditions and say that we must change because conditions are changing.

But I say to you, as God's servant, with the word of the Living God in my mouth, let the weather-vane preachers go around as they please if they want to, but we must have a fixed point for our faith.

A point that will not turn!

A point that will not change!

A point that is absolutely immovable!

120

Our fixed point of faith is not some spiritual trip!

Our fixed point of faith is not a manifestation of some spirit!

Our fixed point of faith is the solid rock of Jesus Christ, the impregnable Word of the Living God!

I don't care how many degrees you have. I don't care what seminary you have been through. I challenge you as God's servant—you cannot have God's faith without God's infallibility.

Now what is our infallibility?

Is it our faith?

No, our infallibility is in the simple Word of the Living God. That is why I love to sing, "On Christ, the solid rock I stand, all other ground is sinking sand." You can't take the fixed points—salvation, healing, the baptism of the Holy Spirit, the second coming of Jesus Christ—you can't take them and let them go around with modern thought and with modern theology. You've got to fix them firm in the infallible Word of God and know that they don't change.

Now there are strange rumblings going on in our land. The Bible has been taken out of the schools. This is only the beginning of troubles in our great nation, a nation which was built on the Word of God. Did you know that witches, wizards, and astrologers are trying to capture our youth? Students say they want classes on the supernatural and on sex, and they are getting them. Research reveals that 92% of our young people are signing up for supernatural courses which are no more than satanic avenues that lead to hell. We take the Bible out; the devil fills the vacuum with demons, witchcraft, wizards, and astrology.

There are strange rumblings in the land, and these

strange rumblings are even cropping up in the old denominations that have been built upon the solid Word of the Living God! There's a great clamor for progress in theology. I appreciate man's trying to extend his mind to a greater depth and understanding of the Word of God. I appreciate this. But when I mark the changing nature of modern opinion, it scares me.

God's Faith Will Change Your Destiny

I am reminded of a thing that recently took place. As I see the terrible curses that face our children, our families, and the people of this generation, I am greatly moved by what I see, because Christians do not know how to combat the evil thoughts and suggestions of the devil with the Word of the Living God.

I had been praying from a distance for some five to six years about a lovely couple. Now I am not talking about general prayer but I am talking about reigning prayer, demanding prayer, persistent prayer that gets answers from the throne of God today. I am talking about the kind of prayer that casts out demons!

The Lord Jesus used this kind of commanding prayer in Mark 5:2-7:

And when he was come out of the ship, immediately there met him out of the tombs a man with an unclean spirit, Who had his dwelling among the tombs; and no man could bind him, no, not with chains: Because that he had been often bound with fetters and chains, and the chains had been plucked asunder by him, and the fetters broken in pieces: neither could any man tame him. And always, night and day, he was in the mountains, and in the tombs, crying and cutting himself with stones. But when he saw Jesus afar off, he ran and worshipped him, And cried with a loud voice, and said, What have I to do with thee, Jesus, thou Son of the most high God? I adjure thee by God, that thou torment me not.

Now obviously Jesus recognized that this man had an unclean spirit, for in verse 8 we read "For Jesus said unto him [the spirit], Come out of the man, thou unclean spirit." What I want you to see is this: the man's strength was supernatural, but it came from demons and devils and not from God. Just because a thing is supernatural doesn't mean it comes from God. And just as the demons then knew Jesus Christ, the Son of God, from afar off, so do demons know the name of Jesus Christ today.

This couple I was praying for had gotten mixed up in witchcraft, witches, wizards, reincarnation. The wife was seeking God. She was zealous; she wanted to serve God with all her heart. But she had gotten sidetracked into satanic cults, not fully realizing that not everything supernatural is good. Consequently, she was bound by demons. Just recently, on a weekend, God moved on my wife and me to start casting out those demons from this woman, just as Jesus cast the demons out of the Gadarene demoniac in Mark 5.

As we prayed, I bound the devil and his forces and commanded them to obey the Word that says, "Behold, I give unto you power ... over all the power of the en-

123

emy" (Luke 10:19); and, "In my name shall they cast out devils" (Mark 16:17).

After we bound the devil and loosed this lady from all those spirits, we felt great peace and victory. The following Tuesday we got a note from her, thanking us with much love for our prayers on her behalf.

On Monday, the day before, this lady had admitted to her husband that she was demonized. After her deliverance she was told by her husband how we had been praying for her, and she responded with the thank-you note.

Now this is the point I am trying to get over to you. All types of people are trying to live in the supernatural. But there is a good supernatural and a bad supernatural. If you choose the bad supernatural, Satan's side, you will become bound like that lady was bound. John 8:34 says, "Whosoever committeth sin is the servant of sin." Make sure you are a servant of God, and not of Satan! Make sure you are on the winning side—God's side! If you are on God's side, if you are a born-again servant of God, I want to show you in this chapter how you can have a supernatural miracle ministry by God's power.

Six Steps to Spiritual Power

I am going to share with you six steps that are a way of life with me. Take these steps and use them, and they will enable you to become a victor over every circumstance. Take this message and preach it, and you will see signs and wonders following your ministry.

ONE: BELIEVE THAT THE BIBLE IS GOD'S VOICE TO US

1) Would you like to hear God talk to you? You can. By simply reading His Word. The Bible in actuality really is God's voice to us.

2) Would you like for God to speak to you in this book? You can listen to the Word of God. I have never asked this question of anyone—man, woman, boy or girl—who has ever said, "No, I don't want to hear the voice of God." People want to hear the voice of God. Now listen very carefully.

3) Ezekiel 12:25, "I am the Lord, I will speak, and the word that I shall speak shall come to pass."

4) Numbers 23:19, "God is not a man, that he should lie; neither the son of man, that he should repent: hath he said, and shall he not do it? or hath he spoken and shall he not make it good?"

5) Can you not hear God speaking to you?

As you accept the authority of the Bible as God's Word to us, your life will be filled with power. As you begin preaching on the validity of God's Word, people will be delivered before you. God honors His Word.

TWO: THE WORD OF GOD IS THE WRITTEN WORD. IT IS ALSO THE LIVING WORD!

We need to understand that God's words are alive. There is life in God's words as we speak them!

In the beginning was the Word, and the Word was with God, and the Word was God. The same

was in the beginning with God. All things were
made by him; and without him was not anything
made that was made ... And the Word was
made flesh, and dwelt among us, (and we beheld
his glory, the glory as of the only begotten of
the Father,) full of grace and truth. [John 1:1,
2,3,14.]

The Word of God is in this book. It is not only the Bible; the Word is also the spirit of Jesus Christ—the Living Resurrection—the Resurrected Son of the Living
God—and He's walking up and down the room wherever you are. The Word of God is alive, and if you are a
born-again Christian, He will never leave you nor for-
sake you.

You cannot separate God from His Word. He *is* His
Word—The Word is God! This Word which made the
beginning, became FLESH! The Word of God is the
Living Word.

Psalm 107:20 says, "He sent his word, and healed
them." The Word of God is with us. The Word of God
is living in us. That Living Word is by your side right
now. Because God is Spirit, He is everywhere present.
The words you speak are like seeds the farmer plants.
Both have their own power to do their own work.
There is miracle life both in the farmer's seed and in
the words we speak.

THREE: THERE IS POWER IN GOD'S SEEDED
WORD
1) Daniel 9:12, "And he hath confirmed his words
... he spake!"

126

2) 1 Peter 1:25, "The word of the Lord endureth forever!"

3) Romans 4:21, "What he had promised, he was able also to perform!"

4) Jeremiah 1:12, "I will hasten my word to perform it!"

The words you speak will germinate seed-faith in the hearts that hear this message. No word of God is void of power. God honors His Word.

How did the disciples work their signs and wonders? I'll tell you how: Christ worked with them! After His Resurrection, and after Jesus was received again into heaven, the disciples "went forth, and preached every where, the Lord working with them, and confirming the word with signs following" (Mark 16:20). The signs followed the Word. There is power in God's seeded Word!

FOUR: GOD'S WORD HAS CREATIVE POWER

The Word of God declares that in the beginning, God created the heavens and the earth. Hebrews tells us that we understand the worlds were created by the word of God.

1) Genesis 1:3, "And God said, Let there be light: and there was light!"

2) Genesis 1:6, 7, "And God said, Let there be a firmament . . . and it was so!"

3) Genesis 1:11, "And God said, Let the earth bring forth grass . . . and it was so!"

On down through the story of creation—

And God said—and God said—each time God spoke, the creative power of His Word went into action!

Out of nothing by the Word of His power.

By His Word God brought into existence the things that are now seen.

There is power in God's Word, creative power.

I am not asking you to look at any gift. I know how easy it is to look at me. You say, "If only the minister will call me out. If only the minister will lay his hand on me." It is not the minister that you need; you just need faith. All you need is to believe, "thus saith the Word of the Living God."

That's all you need!

No more thrills, that's it!

This message is long overdue in America. Too many put their eyes on man rather than standing on the infallibility of "thus saith the Lord." God's Word cannot change. God's Word will not be yea today and nay tomorrow. God is no respecter of persons. My prayer is no better than your prayer. You must act on the Word of God.

FIVE: CHRIST DEMONSTRATED THIS CREATIVE POWER; SO CAN YOU

Even the religious leaders were astonished at the words of authority and power Christ demonstrated through His ministry. And let me tell you something: you can have the same power Jesus had. He said, "Verily, verily, I say unto you, He that believeth on me, the works that I do shall he do also; and greater works than these shall he do; because I go unto my Father" (John 14:12).

One day a boy in the synagogue took ill with fits, and began screaming.

Jesus commanded the unclean spirit to come out of the boy. Immediately the boy was cleansed and in his right mind.

The religious leaders exclaimed, "What a word is this! for with authority and power he commandeth the unclean spirits and they come out" (Luke 4:36).

To the leper He said, "I will, be thou clean" (Matthew 8:3).

Immediately, the creative power of His Word went into action and new flesh began to appear upon the leper.

There is creative power in God's Word.

To the man with the twisted hand in the Temple, He commanded, "Stretch forth thine hand" (Matthew 12:13). Immediately the bad hand became as normal as the other!

There is creative power in God's Word.

Whether it was the leper or the cripple or the blind or the miracle of the wine, there was evidence that the Word of God was being made manifest with creative power.

SIX: FAITH IS SOMETHNG YOU DO.

Faith is an act. Faith in God's Word is acting on God's Word.

One day the Lord told Peter, "Let's go fishing in that lake!" Peter said, in effect, "I have been fishing all night! And there are no fish in that lake! The fish aren't biting!"

In the Sea of Galilee, you don't go fishing in the

daytime, the reason being that it is too crystal clear in the daylight, and the fish see the nets coming down and they scatter.

In the early break of dawn Jesus said, "Let's go and cast out those nets!"

Peter looked at the Master and he said, "Lord, I know there are no fish out there!" He said, "We have toiled all night and taken nothing: nevertheless at thy word I will let down the net." (Read Luke 5.)

Nevertheless at Thy word!

People, isn't it enough for us that God has said it?

Isn't it enough for us that it is written?

Isn't it enough for us that Jesus Christ paid the price for us?

Isn't it enough for us—to believe in the name of Jesus, the Son of the Living God?

Well, let's rise up and believe now in Jesus' name.

"He sent his word and healed them!"

The Living Word, the Resurrected Lord, is in the midst of the people of God.

He is the living truth, and the vibrant stillness of His resurrection glory!

And He shall come by His Spirit!

And shall heal your soul!

And shall lift your discouragement!

And heal your sickness!

And you will walk and reign forevermore in the heavenlies with your God.

Now get ready to do; yes, get ready to do what you couldn't do before, get ready to act your faith. I like to see people act their faith.

I am not going to have you get in a healing line!

Is that all right with you?

You have been through too many lines already; I am going to put something inside of you and underneath you—

It will open up blind eyes—

It will unstop deaf ears—

It will cause cripples to leap up—

It's the power of the Living God. It is the only way God manifests His power, through the seed of faith we plant by preaching.

Faith is action. If you have a bad arm, move it! He took our infirmities and diseases. If He took them, how can you have them? You have them because you think you have to carry them.

You want to get rid of them? Give them to Him! Give them to Him!!!

"Surely he hath borne our griefs and carried our sorrows . . . He was wounded for our transgressions, he was bruised for our iniquities: the chastisement of our peace was upon him" (Isaiah 53:4, 5).

You say, "Oh, Brother Panos, that only refers to spiritual sickness." No, it refers to *any* sickness. I am so glad that God wrote Matthew 8:17, 18, because it is recorded that this verse was fulfilled by Jesus!

So "that it might be fulfilled which was spoken by Esaias the prophet, saying,

"Himself took our infirmities and bare our sicknesses!"

He took our grief and carried our sorrows.

The Bible says He went up and down the streets and He healed the sick and He cast out the devils and He healed all the sick that came unto Him that it might be fulfilled, which was spoken by the prophet.

He took our infirmities—

He bore our sickness!

He took our grief and carried our sorrows!

All right give it to Him, go on give it to Him, give Him that sugar diabetes, give it to Him. Go on and give it to Him, give Him that deaf ear—give Him that blind eye—Go on, give Him that high blood pressure! Give Him that tumor, that cancer.

If you couldn't move those backs, move those legs, the power of God is all over you—the Spirit of the Living God is upon you now as you read this book.

Faith is an act! Move those arms—

Don't play!!

Do it like you mean it.

Deaf mutes, *hear*; the Spirit of the Lord is upon you.

Place your hands on all your sicknesses—all diseases. Say, "Father, I come to You in the name of Jesus Christ. Jesus said, "If you ask anything in my name, that will I do, that the Father may be glorified in the Son" (John 14:13).

Father, glorify Yourself before us. Glorify Yourself right now in these physical bodies!

Satan, you will obey the Word of the Ressurrected Lord, not the words of Chris Panos, but the Word of the Resurrected Lord.

Jesus said, "Behold I give you power . . . over all the power of the enemy"; He said, "In my name ye shall cast out devils."

Satan, you obey the Word of God now in these physical bodies; in the name of Jesus you will take your hands off and loose them *now*.

132

Now, deaf and dumb spirits, obey the Word of the Resurrected Lord. Come out! Go, in Jesus' name.

You foul blind spirits, you that cause darkness on those eyes God's people are praying for, in the name of Jesus be thou gone now! Go!

If you have a deaf ear, put a finger in your good ear and hear! I said hear!

How many who read this book will say, "I know I feel the power of the Holy Spirit. I know God did something for me now!"

Listen to me very carefully, your life has been revolutionized if you've received these words of faith. If you are born again, washed in the blood of Jesus, you may take this message with these six steps and preach this to the crowds, to the nations, to the sick, to the afflicted, *and you will get the same results I am getting now.* If you are teaching Christians how to have miracles in their lives, give them these six steps and instruct them how to make disciples and to preach the Word.

Never in my whole life have I seen so many thousands being saved and healed, as when I started to preach this message. This message has been proven hundreds of times over and it works every time. The destiny of your life will change when you put this message into practice and preach it. My brothers and sisters, put these six spiritual steps to power into action!

CHAPTER 12

COMMANDING FAITH POWER

The people of the world in this age yearn for a demonstration of the power of the Son of the Living God. They long for someone to show them a God Who is powerful to meet them at the level of their problems and to give them an answer.

You that are in bondage to sin or sickness, and you who would liberate men, consider this challenge: "I have chosen you, and ordained you . . . that whatsoever ye shall ask of the Father in my name, he may give it you" (John 15:16).

Looking back and sharing one of the things I heard just after I launched out across the waters into Communist nations, I talked to a man who had been in prison in Communist China. At the beginning of our conversation, this man said, "It's impossible for a foreign missionary to come into China to reach Christians and to preach to them."

The man who was interpreting for me used to be a teacher and pastor. I asked him, "Would there be any chance for a foreign missionary to go into Red China and preach the Gospel to Christians without being arrested?"

He said there were three reasons why he didn't think so. First, it would be impossible to get in. Second, it would be dangerous for the Christians. Third, the missionary would probably be arrested and put into prison.

If I had believed those words, I would never have been able to go to the nations into which I have gone as of today. God never called me just to go to the Christians. When God leads me by the Holy Spirit into these places, I don't look for the Christians.

When I am sent into a nation, I go to preach to the sinners, to the unbelievers, and to those who have never heard of the wonderful Gospel of Jesus Christ. These are the ones who need to know about the blood of Jesus that cleanses us from all unrighteousness.

I tell them, "God so loved the world, that he gave his only begotten Son, that whosoever believeth in him should not perish, but have everlasting life" (John 3:16).

The Apostle Paul didn't play around when he bound the eyes of Elymas the Sorcerer (Acts 13:11).

Paul acted on God's Word. He did it. He didn't pray. He went straight forward. *Faith is the daring of the soul to go further than it can see.* That's the power of God. That's commanding faith power; but we must dare to rise up and use it.

When we pray in this manner, we demand answers. This is not to take away from what these precious

135

Chinese brethren were saying. But their minds were captivated with ministering to Christians, and they felt the bonds and restrictions under which Communism had placed them.

There's no doubt but that the Christians need encouragement. But God has led me in a peculiar way in bamboo curtain countries. (And when I say bamboo curtain countries, I refer to those linked with Red China: North Vietnam, some of Cambodia, some of Thailand, North Korea and some of Indonesia.)

When I refer to those countries, people think it's impossible to take the Gospel there. But many thousands of New Testaments in the New Chinese are being taken into Red China. God is raising up surrendered vessels everywhere who are willing to DIE, not only to die to self, but to let the body itself die and be literally crucified, if need be, to take the Gospel into that country.

That is a consecrated walk! One that is willing to do ALL THINGS!

You can praise God for the rest of your life. You can stay in your churches, you can go to camp meetings, you can get together with the brethren and they can prophesy and say that you're holy before God. But God's great commission in this hour is to "Go ye into all the world, and preach the gospel to every creature" (Mark 16:15). "Every creature" is estimated to number FOUR BILLION souls by 1975. Right now, this instant, there are ONE BILLION souls in the iron and bamboo curtain countries without the Gospel.

The Lord is looking for men and women who are willing to lay hold of the Word of the Living God and to carry the battle against the enemy in the hard places.

136

Joshua laid hold of the Word of the Living God. In his battle against the enemy, he commanded the sun and the moon to stand still. These are the works of God's hands. No one had ever dared to try this before. Joshua had a need, and he believed God's Word; so with the audacity of naked faith, he commanded the sun and the moon to stand still. The whole solar system came to a halt while God wrought a great deliverance for Israel.

Joshua delivered the people of God, and God wrote Joshua's name among the men of faith.

I can go to testimony after testimony where God has honored His Word in response to the command of faith.

In Mexico, when I had gone with other missionaries to preach at a mountaintop village, the day had been bright and shining. But when it came time to preach, a cold wind joined with stormy rain clouds to threaten the open-air meeting.

I commanded the wind and rain to go. I told the cold air to be gone in the name of Jesus, by the authority of the Word of God, so the people would be able to come and hear the Gospel.

It came to pass!

Did God invest all of his power in Brother Panos? Does Brother Panos have a corner on the truth? God forbid!

Joshua *could* have prayed, but the Bible doesn't mention anything about his praying. It *does* say that he commanded.

There is a time to pray, and there is also a time to act. There is a time for praying, and there is a time for commanding. Prayer without action is words without faith. Get faith.

Jesus did much praying. When there was a need for action, He acted. When the ship was about to sink on the stormy Sea of Galilee, Jesus awoke to find frightened disciples. He walked up on the deck where the winds and waves were blowing. He stood still and simply said, "Peace, be still" (Mark 4:39).

Suddenly, there was peace—complete silence and stillness.

Did nature hear the commanding voice of Jesus Christ, the Son of the Living God? Did the sun and the moon hear the voice of Joshua? Yes, they did. The commanding power of faith is always heard.

I remember in 1966 when I was on my way to a camp meeting at a Bible institute. On my way there by airplane, God had spoken to me to go back and pray for some people.

Frankly, I wanted to go on to be with my brethren, to hear and give testimonies, to hear preaching and to preach. I had no desire to go pray for this couple. But God was concerned. And He had chosen me to do it.

As I was on the airplane, the Lord spoke to my heart, "Son, I wish you had stayed and prayed for this couple."

I said, "Lord, You know what I want to do. You know the desires of my heart."

He said, "Son, I know. But you must go back."

I said, "Lord, how can I go back?"

He answered, "Command the airplane to turn around and go back."

I asked Him again. He said yes.

With a deep sigh, I turned around and silently bound

the airplane and commanded it to turn and go back. Then I turned to the man sitting next to me, and told him what I had done by way of testimony.

Immediately, something took place. We were arriving at the city where we were to land. I looked out, and the fog was so dense you couldn't see anything. The pilot came on the intercom and told us we would be unable to land because of the visibility.

There was enough gas to go on to the next town, or to go back where we came from. Because I had obeyed God's voice (and for no other reason), a miracle took place. The airplane turned around and went back!

Moses obeyed the voice of God when he stretched out his rod across the Red Sea, and it parted just as God had said it would. I obeyed the voice of God in the airplane, and the airplane turned around.

When we're in the place where we ought to be, and God speaks to us, and we command and obey in the name of Jesus, what we say will come to pass. And it will happen not because we're infallible, but because God's Word is infallible.

The Bible says in Matthew 21:19: "And when he saw a fig tree ... he came to it, and found nothing thereon, but leaves only, and said unto it, Let no fruit grow on thee henceforward for ever. And presently the fig tree withered away."

Jesus said, "Verily I say unto you, If ye have faith, and doubt not, ye shall not only do this which is done to the fig tree, but also if ye shall say unto this mountain, Be thou removed, and be thou cast into the sea; it shall be done" (Matthew 21:21).

The Gospel has never changed. When the Lord sent out His disciples to preach the Gospel, the power of

God unto salvation, He gave them instructions. You may say, "What do you mean, 'instructions'?"

"Heal the sick, cleanse the lepers, raise the dead, cast out devils: freely ye have received, freely give" (Matthew 10:8).

Jesus wants to set His people free.

Not too long ago a man was resurrected in South America. He had been killed in a fall from a telephone pole. Men gathered around and prayed, and commanded his resurrection. For them it happened the same way it did for Peter when he prayed for Dorcas, or Tabitha. It happened the same way it did for Paul when he was "long preaching" and a man fell from the second floor window. (It would have been a miracle if he hadn't broken his neck!) But Eutychus was raised to life at the command of Paul.

When Jesus commissioned the seventy and commanded them to go, He said, "Whatsoever city ye enter, and they receive you, eat such things as are set before you: And heal the sick that are therein, and say unto them, The kingdom of God is come nigh unto you" (Luke 10:8, 9).

Do you see the place of power where we stand? When you read, notice how many times the disciples used this commanding power. They were not praying for the sick, they were delivering the sick! "If ye have faith, and doubt not, ye shall not only do this which is done to the fig tree, but also if ye shall say unto this mountain, Be thou removed, and be thou cast into the sea; it shall be done" (Matthew 21:21).

This is not done through a false sense of importance. It doesn't come to pass by being little "gods," by running around and shouting, and shaking everything and everybody, becoming great in our own eyes. When you come to understand how to heal the sick and drive out disease, it will give you a sense of humility and utter dependence on God, Who is the source of all power.

If you are drowning, and I cast you a lifesaver attached to the rope and draw you safely in, what would you say saved you? You might declare that the lifesaver saved you, or that the rope didn't break, and it saved you, but really it would be the one who threw it and pulled you out who saved you. Jesus is the only one Who is able to save. We only act as the rope.

So we take the Gospel into Communist nations, going through customs, going to preach through interpreters who are Communist spies. You know it and they know it, but so does Jesus! Like the lifesaver or the rope, we are only the instrument of deliverance. Behind it all is God and His mighty love and mercy.

Mightier is our God than all the noises of many waters. Mightier is our God than all the sicknesses, than all the nations, than all the ballistic missiles, than all of China with its teeming hordes of numberless humanity, and all of Russia.

God tells us to heal the sick. We do this either by taking something out of people, like a surgeon does, or by putting something into them. We must get out that sin which hinders the power of God through unbelief, and put in the message of the Cross and the promises of the Living God.

We must sow good seed, and it's only sown as the Word is preached.

The reason why you don't see too many healings in camp meetings is that men don't know how to preach the Gospel. The Lord sent His disciples out to preach, and He told them what to do.

Believers are also given power in this last day. The disciples were not going merely with instructions to pray for the sick. They were given power to heal the sick. That's what Peter and John did in Acts 3. They acted on what Jesus told them to do.

Peter said simply, "Silver and gold have I none; but such as I have give I thee: In the name of Jesus Christ of Nazareth rise up and walk. And he took him by the right hand, and lifted him up: and immediately his feet and ancle bones received strength. And he leaping up stood, and walked, and entered with them into the temple, walking, and leaping, and praising God" (Acts 3:6-8). Jesus said, "I give you power." "Heal the sick." "Cast out devils." One of the gifts of the Spirit is the gift of healing. Another is the gift of miracles. Jesus instructed us to heal the sick. On all occasions Jesus healed the sick. He is our example.

Jesus never prayed for the sick. He *commanded* the sickness to go. No one ever walked on the water, or commanded the sun to stand still, or stopped the mouths of lions, or quenched the violence of fire with a half-hearted attitude.

The world's lord may lead you into want, into pain, into heartache, but my Lord leads to green pastures.

The centurion told the Lord that he didn't need to come to his house for his servant to be healed. You don't have to pray. Just speak the Word. "I am a man under authority, having soldiers under me: and I say to this man, Go, and he goeth; and to another, Come, and he cometh; and to my servant, Do this, and he doeth it" (Matthew 8:9). What he meant was, "Lord, You're

142

the same kind of man. Your authority is not over the Roman soldiers. It's over infirmity, over the works of the devil. Your authority is over sickness and sin. Lord, You stand right here and speak the word only and there's not enough sin to hold my servant in captivity. There's not enough power to hold back the healing power of the Son of God!"

We heal the sick by giving them the Word of God just as Jesus spoke the Word to the centurion.

Notice that Jesus first says, "Go preach. (Or, go teach, and give out the Word of God.) Then heal the sick, cleanse the lepers, cast out devils." This Scripture says He gave them power over unclean spirits to cast them out, and to heal all manner of sicknesses, all manner of diseases.

Where is this power? How do we get it to work?

The Bible says to preach it. Teach it. Give it out. "Freely ye have received, freely give" (Matthew 10:8). Bless God, you can give the imperishable Word of the Living God and then the words you speak will be the words of Jesus.

That's the commanding power that God wants us to have in this latter day. The power is the Word of the Living God.

The Gospel is the power of God unto salvation to everyone that believeth, whether he is Red Chinese, Red Russian, or from one of the Red satellite countries. Wherever he might be, the Word of God is the power of God unto salvation.

Through the power of preaching, men are brought to repentance. When they repent and give up their sin, *something is taken out* of their hearts. When they receive Jesus and His promises into their hearts, they are able to receive the Gospel, the power of God INTO their hearts, so *something is added.*

If you have the Gospel, you have the power. If you give the Gospel, you give the power. Without the Word, you have no power. Without Me, Jesus said, ye can do nothing. You don't *pray* for the power of God, you *give* the power of God—you give the Gospel.

A perfect picture of this occurs in Acts 14.

When the cripple was present in one of the services of Paul the apostle, Paul preached and gave forth the Word faithfully. Then he perceived (realized) the cripple had received faith to be healed. The Word produced faith.

Paul saw his faith and commanded him to stand up and walk. A miracle took place. The man was healed. Paul healed him. How did he do it? By teaching him what God did through the sacrifice of Jesus.

The promises of God produce repentance and faith, setting into action the Word of God. Behind it all is the Source—the Power of God, our merciful Heavenly Father.

I've seen this happen many times.

In one place I preached, a little girl who was insane was brought to the meeting. She heard the Gospel. But she was still spewing and spitting, and looking cross-eyed. But the love of God which passes all understanding reached out to her through me. I clutched her to my bosom. She bit my chest. She looked horrible. I wanted to leave her and that place too. But I released her in the name of Jesus, and a few moments later she was as sane and whole as she possibly could be.

The Gospel, the power of God unto salvation, set

144

her free. I've seen it happen. You can preach, but unless you preach the Gospel, the power of God unto salvation, the words are as sounding brass and tinkling cymbals.

It's only the Word of God that sets humanity free. God is faithful. He works through His Word. No Word of God shall be void of power. The Words of God are "life unto those that find them, and health to all their flesh" (Proverbs 4:22).

Go forth as Jesus commanded. YOU heal the sick. YOU cast out devils. YOU cleanse the lepers. Jesus said, I give this power to YOU.

Exercise this power in the name of Jesus. Healing and deliverance come through His Word, through the Word of the Living God.

Give out the Word. It is the power of the Living God.

When the people hear and understand the Gospel, and repent, turning to Jesus, their sicknesses and troubles have to leave. Teach them to command them to leave in the name of Jesus. The sicknesses will have to go, because it is the Word of God.

When you give this command, you will not be speaking; it will be Christ who dwells in you. Therefore you cannot fail. You can arise in your Redeemer and say to every mountain, "Be thou removed."

Use this commanding faith in the name of Jesus, and God will use you as His sharp threshing instrument to bring forth the precious grain of His harvest.

It can't be reiterated too often, "Faith is the daring of the soul to go further than it can see." As you lay your life on the line to be used of God in the work of telling those who don't know Him about Jesus, claim the promises of God and remember always that you haven't seen anything yet.

We are now ready to consider the greatest lesson of all. May God the Holy Spirit open our hearts to receive it in its fullness.

CHAPTER 13

GET READY FOR THE HARVEST

The Lord has spoken to me afresh, and as I sat down to write this chapter I heard this message loud and clear: "Go Forward! Son, I am getting ready to work marvels, miracles that will supersede any other period of time, including the time of the early Church. Yes, I am pouring out My Spirit upon all flesh! Get ready for the biggest harvest of souls, for the hour has arrived!"

As I sit and write to you, the very air is impregnated with the supernatural love of Jesus Christ. The following message is given in love to caution all who will be used in this mighty move of God to do His works in these last days.

147

The Real Armor

Our story opens with a shepherd boy named David. I believe that in his early days, David's ambitions never soared higher than the humble job committed to him. The birthright belonged to the firstborn, whereas David was the youngest of Jesse's eight sons.

But when the Lord repented that He had made Saul king over Israel and decided to choose another king in his stead, He passed by all those seemingly best fitted for the job and searched among those apparently least "likely to succeed" for Saul's replacement. So the Lord sent his prophet, Samuel, to Bethlehem, to anoint a king from among the sons of Jesse. Tongues wagged and ears tingled as the prophet journeyed into Bethlehem, "And the elders of the town trembled at his coming and said, Comest thou peaceably?" They couldn't understand what ministry would bring God's prophet to their little town. Led by God, Samuel went to the house of Jesse and called for Jesse's sons to be brought before him. One by one, Jesse had seven of his sons pass before Samuel, and when Samuel chose none of them, he had them all pass by again. But Samuel said to Jesse, "The Lord hasn't chosen these." He asked if Jesse didn't have another son.

In effect, Jesse replied, "Well, there's my youngest— but he's just a shepherd." Jesse couldn't understand what the Lord would want with such a young boy— and a shepherd boy at that!

But Samuel, having a better understanding of the

ways of the Lord, said, "Send and fetch him!" So they brought David, and as he stood before God's prophet, the Lord said, "Arise, anoint him, for this is he." Then the anointing oil was poured out on him and David the shepherd boy was destined to be king. (Read 1 Samuel 16.)

Strong Yet Weak

Thus God sometimes stoops down and picks out a Gypsy Smith, a Robert Moffat, a nobody He is going to fill with the glory of His presence and send forth into the world to be kings in the realms of the Spirit. You remember David had already had two thrilling experiences (experience always comes before greater service), for in the strength of the Lord he had slain the lion and killed the bear. God saw he could trust David, for God looks at the steadfastness of our allegiance to the truth, at the way we react and respond to the little things our hands find to do. It is upon the head of the man who has been found faithful, that the anointing oil is poured. (Cheer up, God is going to use you!) The more important the work envisioned, the more you need to apply yourself with all your might to even the most unimportant task you have at hand.

Remember that the way we tackle the seemingly insignificant problems and tasks of our spiritual life is what we are putting before God to look at and to judge us by. And so David (because he had already had experience with the lion and with the bear; because he had been not faithless, but believing) was destined to be led by the Spirit of God into new vistas of service that he had never dreamed of in his boyhood days! I want to introduce you to the boy who marched onto the battlefield and heard the words of Goliath as he defied the armies of the Living God. David had this confidence, that if any man would go forth, God would not suffer that man to be defeated. All of Israel knew God *could* kill Goliath, but only one, the shepherd boy, believed God *would* do it.

The Real Armor

In 1 Samuel 17, we find the story of how Goliath defied the whole army of Israel, crying, "Give me a man that we may fight together," and how all the men of Israel, when they saw Goliath, fled from him and were afraid; and the men of Israel said to David, "Have ye seen this man that is come up?"

"And David spake." (What you *say* is what you get!) He said, "What shall be done to the man that killeth this Philistine and taketh away the reproach from Israel? for who is this uncircumcised Philistine, that he should defy the armies of the living God?" (verse 26). You remember Saul's saying, "thou art but a youth, and he a man of war from his youth" (verse 33). And David spoke a second time, saying, "Thy servant slew both the lion and the bear; and this uncircumcised Philistine shall be as one of them . . . moreover, The LORD that delivered me out of the paw of the lion and out of the paw of the bear, he will deliver me out of the hand of this Philistine" (verses 36, 37). And so he chose five smooth stones out of the brook and put them in his bag.

And thus little David went forth to face this Hercules of the opposite army, after laying aside the armor of Saul! Saul's armor didn't feel right. It was useless to David, for he was accustomed to God's weapons instead of the armor of the world: "For the weapons of our warfare are not carnal, but mighty through God to the pulling down of strongholds" (2 Corinthians 10:4). We cannot fight the world with worldly swords and worldly spears, worldly guns and worldly ways. (Listen—I am speaking to you—we do not use the world's ways to get or to fight our enemies.)

The ministry of every Spirit-filled believer, baptized into the Church, the body of Christ, is a ministry identical to the ministry of Christ. For as God was in Christ, reconciling the world to Him, so Christ is in us carrying on the work of reconciliation; and our most powerful weapon is love!

The most potent things Christ used were the weakest things, and the weakest things were the strongest! "A soft answer turneth away wrath" (Proverbs 15:1). "Vengeance is mine; I will repay, saith the Lord" (Romans 12:19).

If your enemy comes against you and you want to overcome him, don't fight him; but if he is hungry, give him food; and if he is thirsty, give him drink. You say that is weakness? No, my brother, THAT IS STRENGTH! My weakness is made perfect in God's strength!

So David put aside Saul's armor, took five stones and went forth with a battle cry on his lips—a battle cry uttered in faith never fails to bring results when we go

151

forth against the Goliaths of our souls! Every one of us has to face "giants" who defy the armies of the Living God. But listen carefully: we cannot win unless we fight God's way, with weapons of God's own choosing, according to God's own plan! David cried out, "Thou comest to me with a sword, and with a spear, and with a shield: but I come to thee in the name of the LORD of hosts, the God of the armies of Israel, whom thou hast defied."

David said, "This day ... I will smite thee, and take thine head from thee ... and all ... shall know that the LORD saveth not with sword and spear;" [I say unto you, Israel, not with jets and missiles, but by my Spirit, saith the Lord of hosts] "for the battle is the LORD'S and he will give you into our hands" (verses 45, 46, 47). Praise God, the battle is the Lord's, my friends, we can conquer in the name of Jesus! There is power in that name! Every one of us has this power in us.

Romanian Customs

The power that we have works just as well today as it did in Bible times. I remember as I boarded a flight from Vienna to Bucharest, I was seated next to a neatly dressed English gentleman named Mr. Potter. A conversation broke out between us. "What is your occupation?" he asked. And I told him quickly as the Holy Spirit spoke through me, "I smuggle God's Bibles into the Communist nations." I asked him, "What do you do?" He was a technical sales representative of Uni-Royal from England. He said, "I am an athiest, but something tells me you are really different." "I want to warn you to be careful," he went on, "They are checking every piece of luggage thoroughly at customs, because there has been a robbery and several famous paintings have been smuggled out through customs." I thanked him for the information, told him that God would cause me to conquer in the name of Jesus. I had power to bind; power to loose; power to set free; not my power but the power of Jesus.

The plane landed and we proceded through customs and just as he said, they were thoroughly investigating all luggage. I was fully loaded with illegal Gospels and New Testaments. Mr. Potter walked before me looking back at me. They opened his bags first; then as they approached me, I bound and "blinded" them in the name of Jesus Christ. They said, "Is this your bag?" I said yes. They said, "Are you with him?" I said yes. They said, "Pass on through." Every one of us must walk in the perfect will of God and use God's weapons and use God's means. If we are careful to do this, we will always "slay" both the physical enemies that face us, and the enemies of our souls.

What happened to Mr. Potter? He was shocked. He could not understand how God used me, or how God delivered me. As we journeyed together to the Lido Hotel in Bucharest he said, "You know every bag, every suitcase, was examined on that air flight, but yours! You almost persuade me to believe that there is a God." Eventually, Mr. Potter wept his way to Christ.

Yes, praise God, every Goliath will go down to defeat before the smallest, weakest child of God, as he speaks the name of Jesus. This is that victory that overcomes the world, even your faith. Faith is the victory!

153

But I believe David was able to do what he did, and I was able to march through Romanian customs as I did, because of the anointing of God's Holy Spirit, and because the holiness of God was rooted and grounded in our hearts.

Success Is Very Dangerous

THE PINNACLE is the greatest danger point I know. The higher up you mount, the farther the distance you can fall. The higher up you are, the more obvious your falls. There is very little danger of falling in the valley. (There is not half the danger of falling in the valley that there is of falling on the mountaintop.)

While you are still in the valley there is nowhere to fall, but as you attain almost to the very height of your Christian experience, it means something to plunge downward to the bottom. It involves an act of being cut off and laid aside! It involves defilement! (I do not believe in romances with someone else's wife or any type of flirtation: sin is sin, whether it be a lie, a robbery, or a romance—apart from a romance with God's Word.) "Stolen bread seems sweet only for awhile, then it becomes death!" (See Proverbs 20:17.)

God will have no fellowship and communion with a defiled saint, though He will cleanse him if he repents and *confesses* his sin. Listen to me, Christian friends, it means something "To keep under my body, lest that by any means, having preached to others, I myself should be a castaway" (1 Corinthians 9:27).

You may not agree with me or with all I say, but if

154

you are to be *used* in the *greatest move God has ever shown on this earth* it's going to cost you something! I know nothing so pitifully tragic that could happen to a minister, or to a man or a woman who is walking with God, as to plunge (after God had blessed him with a successful ministry), from the very pinnacle of the success to which he had been elevated! Hurled down by spiritual pride, by self-will acting apart from God, by committing adultery with the world, by offering strange fire or strange incense, or like Saul, even lying nine times to God, offering sacrifice instead of obedience! Nothing is so pitiful as when the very success attained becomes a curse because of our sensual, devilish, fleshly pride. For *a man or woman is only tempted when he is led away of his own lusts and enticed!*

While we are humble, while we are melted, while we are broken, while we are empty, *God can use us.* We must watch our success just as much as we watch our seeming defeats and failures. By experience I have found out that the hard place is not the hard place, it is the secure place. When things are progressing well, then I am driven to my knees, for when everything is going smoothly there is a tendency to let down, to take things as a matter of course; but when the storm clouds gather, and the rain descends, and the floods come and the winds blow, we begin to dwindle. In times of trouble our self-esteem and our self-conceit vanish and we begin to feel we are not quite so much. (Some say, "Brother Panos, don't preach this way, you cannot have any friends this way. Let's skip, jump, and have a merry time, we are saved by grace." But friends, the grace of God is not a license to sin.) Let me share with you that the way up is down. God can make a king out of a shepherd boy as long as he will keep the shepherd boy spirit. The time of David's troubles came when he reached the very pinnacle of success, when the people cried out, "Saul has slain his thousands, and David his ten thousands!" (1 Samuel 18:7). I can imagine David as he walked the streets, with the crowds yelling their approval and clapping their hands hour after hour. Listen to me: it went to David's head!

David began to number the people. (Now how many prophets in the U.S.A. say, "My, I had several thousands of people out tonight and every person I touched fell to the ground"; David did much the same thing.) There is a wrong way to do right, and *too much David* and not enough of God came to the surface, more and more often. Then God said, "David, I have a service for you to perform; I want you to bring back the ark." Listen to me, thousands get saved overseas. One night 187 cripples rose up and walked all in one service. The crowds went wild. They clapped their hands. Don't tell me you don't feel it. Forty thousand souls were swept into the kingdom of God. People in the U.S.A. are falling under the power of God. Listen to me, when things are going well it is easy to get our eyes on the manifestations and the crowds, I don't care who you are or how long you have been preaching.

There Is Danger in Success

Let us watch our success. A man does not have to be backslidden to the extent that he has gone clear back in the world. No sir, he can still use the Scripture terms and go on preaching, he can still have no difference to speak of in form, and yet have lost that keen touch with God. The principle and the method may be right, and the motive may be wrong. God dealt with a worm named Gideon this way: God can take a worm, a plowboy, and make him a prophet of God.

Now there is coming soon another King, who is going to rule on David's throne, and that King is from the lineage of David, and His name is Jesus. You want to be really used of God? Humble yourself; seek God. Oh, what big things God can do with little people! What mighty things God can do with human beings! God is infusing the Body of Christ with the greatest anointing of all times, one that will supersede the early Church a hundredfold: marvels and miracles of all kinds are upon us. You have not seen anything yet.

God spoke to me in an audible voice recently and every fiber of my being was electrified.

Even the air was electric.

He said, "Son, the greatest outpouring has just begun to be released!"

He said, "You have not begun to see what I am going to do!"

I say this in the right attitude, because I am thrilled with what God said to me: "You have not seen anything yet!"

As the Holy One spoke my thoughts seemed to project a vision before me: I saw the miraculous escapes through customs; I watched the "blinding" of the guards' eyes in Communist nations; I observed the many great miracles God had already performed for me!

157

Like dropping the 135° weather in New Delhi to 98° immediately after prayer, just by mentioning the name of Jesus. I picked up the paper the next day and read an article which said that such a sudden change had never before taken place. I saw visions of past miraculous escapes. I saw many of my past experiences, like the miracle campaigns in many nations. I saw giant crusades where tens of thousands had gathered together to be saved under the preaching of the mighty Word of God.

As I perceived these triumphs in the spirit, my heart seemed to break forth with such great joy to think, "I haven't seen anything yet!"

God said: "I am going to send you to the four corners of the Earth proclaiming my message!"

Then a sea of people seemed to focus before my naked eyes and it was as if I were looking out of a telescope. I saw Indian souls, Japanese souls, African, Jewish, Chinese, German, Greek, Thai, and Austrian souls.

I saw nearly every tribe in this enormous sea of people.

God said, "Son, thou hast been faithful over a little; now I will usher you into one of the last phases of your ministry."

He said to tell my people to get ready for the biggest harvest of souls ever presented upon the face of this earth. Then I began to speak—

I was trembling and I began to speak from my spirit for some thirty to forty minutes. The answers to many promises that I had prayed for, and many visions and prayers that I was praying about for myself and my directors' interests and our Far East Reporter Family seemed to be revealed to me.

God told me many things that would happen; He told me He was going to bless our directors exceeding abundantly above all that I had asked or even thought.

God told me of a fresh new oil of gladness, a new anointing of wisdom, of knowledge, and of power that would be manifested as never before in our ministry.

Then God said: "Son, you will raise up a host of American evangelists and teach them how to preach the Gospel to sinners overseas as you yearned for someone to teach you. And you will be moved in this last day to raise tens of thousands of nationals and they will come forth out of your ministry.

God told me that I would have a two-fold duty: first I would teach the American evangelists, and second, I would raise the nationals up to reach their own people and teach them how to raise up their own evangelists as I had already been doing, only now it would reach into the thousands.

God told me many things that space will not allow me to share with you. But let me close my little testimony with this statement: you too are going to be ushered into a last-day ministry that will supersede your wildest dreams and hopes. God told me that Christians would go forth in a greater ministry than at any other period of time! I promise you your life will rocket into new dimensions as you go forth in the name of Christ. Expect it: your best days are ahead of you. Jesus is coming very soon.

CHAPTER 14

YOU HAVEN'T BEGUN TO SEE ANYTHING YET!

E ye hath not seen, nor ear heard, neither have entered into the heart of man, the things which God hath prepared for them that love him" (1 Corinthians 2:9). There is not a doubt in my mind, in my spirit, or in my faith life, that we are on the verge of the most unusual outpouring of the Holy Spirit that the world has ever seen.

Acts 2:17 says, "And it SHALL come to pass." It doesn't say it *might* come to pass; it doesn't say it *would* come to pass *if* God could convert some skeptics to believe it. The Bible says it *shall* come to pass. In the last days, saith God, "I will pour out of my spirit upon all flesh."

Some think we have seen all that God is ever going to do. If we have already seen all that God has for us, then we have relegated ourselves to being useless occupiers of territory held mainly by the devil. I don't believe that any generation, including those of Moses, the prophet Elijah, Elisha, the apostles, or any of the revivals of modern days, has yet begun to see what God has prepared for us when He begins His last-day outpouring of the Holy Ghost.

We haven't yet begun to see what God is going to do for us!

Some people have the idea that God can't speak to people today. Just because their lines of communication have been broken for so long, they don't think God can speak to anybody. I've got news for you, brother, God speaks to people. He speaks to people the same way He did to Elijah, the same way He did to Elisha, right here in this modern twentieth century.

We are living in the last days. I don't think there's a man or a woman or a young person reading this book now who is truly and sincerely right with God in his heart, who isn't conscious that Jesus Christ is coming soon. God said, "In the last days, it shall come to pass." I know when we look around about us in the United States of America, there doesn't seem to be much hope for revival.

The pleasures of this world have gripped the American people. They are losing their God-consciousness and their fear of God, and they have turned to the pleasures of this world. There isn't anything that describes the conditions of the people of the United States of America as vividly as this!

Furthermore, the divorce laws are lax. Is it hard to get a divorce today? Free sex is rampant everywhere. It was this way fifty years ago, before the last great revival. At that time, gambling was at a high rate. Murder reached its peak. All of these are parallel conditions to those in which America finds itself today.

In 1966 and 1967, mobs ruled our cities. More recently we have had the 1972 presidential incident, more violence in our streets, and Watergate.

Unless something happens in the United States of America in the next few years, what happened a few years ago in Detroit will look like child's play. There are plans under way to burn down great areas of U.S. cities. People are hoping for mob rule! Mob administration! Mob violence!

We have listened to "God is dead" theology in the United States of America! Clergy who know no spirit of dignity take the Word of God in their hands and sit around press tables and say that God is dead, that He's a myth!

Throughout our entire history, Americans have strayed from the paths of righteousness. But I'll tell you something: "Where sin abounded, grace did much more abound" (Romans 5:20).

In the mid-1800's Americans had opened themselves up to the introduction of influential free thinkers like Thomas Paine and other European infidels who saturated American philosophy with their trash. But something happened. The Holy Spirit of the Living God began to brood over this nation. Conviction of sin began to grip the people in their moment and hour of desperation, in the midst of their chaos. People began to reach out. They began to cry and to plead with God. A full-scale revival broke out that swept this entire country. In New York City alone, 5,000 people a day would gather in special prayer meetings. Great prayer meetings began to spring up everywhere.

This revival was so strong that it developed a peculiar kind of emphasis. People coming into the United States of America on passenger ships would fall under the power of God on the ship, because conviction would settle so strongly on them. They didn't understand why. They got saved coming into this country, and when they got here, they found out that there was a mighty Holy Ghost revival on. The Holy Spirit began to work inside the taverns until taverns in many places had to close their doors, as proprietors began to sell out to the blood-stained banner of the cross.

Spiritual epidemics broke out in the revival in the mid-1800's. When Spurgeon wrote about it, he wrote conservatively, temperately, and by good authority. He said that there were whole towns in New England where you couldn't find one unconverted person—not one! That's how great the revival power was. Beloved, I want you to know something. When the true Holy Ghost revival power and fire of God comes again, it'll do just exactly that.

What a unique revival it was! Inside a factory, people would be working at their machines. Suddenly, the Holy Ghost would come inside that factory, and they would have to close down the whole floor and start a prayer meeting because the power of God was so strong that many would be slain under the power. People were getting saved everywhere without a preacher. And something happened to the preachers—they weren't so stiff and starchy anymore. They lost their stiffness and their starchiness, and they lost it in a mighty big hurry. They went on their faces before God; they began to cry, to repent, to beg God's forgiveness; they began to get right with Him. They took the Word of the Living God in

163

their hands and began to preach it fearlessly! They began to believe the Bible as they had never believed it before.

In 1929, there was another great revival, preceded by a period of great sin and immorality. Fifty years ago, there was a tremendous rise of false cults that gripped this nation. One of the leading cults was spiritualism! People were delving into demon practice—just as they are today. Why? Because they had no eternal faith in a living, resurrected Christ. And whenever you lose your faith in Christ, you'll turn to spiritualist mediums and astrology and fortune telling—all of which are abominations to the Lord. (Read 2 Kings 23.)

Even the clergy of America, strange as it may seem, have turned in our day to spiritualist mediums. One man, a leading bishop of a big organization, was so bold as to appear on television a few years back in Toronto, to state that he had communications with his dead son. But strange as it may seem to those who don't know the Lord, he got lost and he died in the desert in the Holy Land.

Let's go back to 1929: fifty years ago, America was generally prosperous. Great airlines began making cross-country flights in a matter of hours. Waterways were opened up. Towns and cities and villages began to spring up everywhere. And the boom was on. That boom included prosperity, pleasure, drunkenness, crime, and free sex!

But something happened; there came to America the greatest time of economic instability that this country had ever known. Banks closed overnight. Wealthy people became paupers. Everyone was in financial distress. Unemployment reached everywhere; you couldn't beg, borrow, or steal a job. But even in the midst of this chaos, the Holy Spirit of the Living God began to brood over this nation, just as it had in the mid-1800's.

Out of the depression came the great heroes of the twentieth-century faith movement; a little woman called Aimee Semple MacPherson, the great giant of a man called Smith Wigglesworth, and probably one of the princes of them all, Dr. Charles Price. His ministry produced hundreds of preachers. In one meeting, fifty people leaped out of wheelchairs. In another meeting in Victoria, Dr. Price prayed for people with cancers, with goiters, and with tumors. They say they had to stop the healing several times to scoop up the goiters and the tumors that were vomited up by the people as he was ministering to over 600 people in one healing line with these conditions.

Just before Charles Price died he said, "Oh, that God would give this preacher the opportunity to see in the physical what I see in the spirit, because I see coming on the horizon, a mighty Holy Ghost revival that will supersede anything that I have ever seen in my ministry. There is coming a move of the Holy Ghost that will be greater than anything I have ever seen!"

If America is going to taste revival, it's going to have to begin with the clergy. If America is going to have any hope for a moving of the Holy Spirit, something is going to have to happen to the preachers. Listen to what Joel says (in Joel 1:11-13):

Be ye ashamed, O ye husbandmen; howl, O ye vine-dressers, for the wheat and for the barley; because the harvest of the field is perished . . . . Gird yourselves, and lament, ye priests. Howl, ye ministers of the altar: come, lie all night in sackcloth, ye ministers of my God: for the meat offering and the drink offering is withholden from the house of your God.

I wonder if there is a preacher in this world today that could dare stand up and say, "Brother Panos, I'm satisfied with what my ministry, my church, was able to accomplish in my community this year."

We need revival. I don't think there is a more desperate people on the face of the earth than we are. We need a moving of the Holy Ghost. And we don't need just something that we've had for a long time—a whoop and a dance, a message in tongues and an interpretation. I'm talking about *revival*—a Holy Ghost revival.

Isn't it strange that God would take economic failure to turn the hearts of His people towards Him? Oh, God, I hope we're not headed down that same road again.

God has told me that we're in the midst of His greatest move right now. God said, "It *shall* come to pass." God didn't say it might come to pass. He said, "It shall come to pass." He said, "I will pour out of my spirit upon all flesh." We are in the midst of a great revival. We are going to see very peculiar kinds of manifestations in this revival.

First of all, we're going to see a revival that knows no limits. In our minds, we have limited an unlimited God. We've limited an unlimited God because we do not see Him as He is. The time is coming—it's already here. People are beginning to wait in God's presence. People are beginning to fast before God. People are beginning to get hold of the horns of the altar and they are waiting in the presence of the Almighty. They are beginning to see Him in a way that they have never seen Him before. There will be no limit to this revival. It will be a revival of the supernatural but there won't

166

be any lack. We won't just happen to hit one miracle somewhere down the line in a healing line. There aren't going to be any boundaries on this revival. Nobody's going to get a corner on it. Not the Baptists, not the Methodists, not the Presbyterians, nor the Episcopalians, and not the Pentecostals. Not the Greek Orthodox nor the Roman Catholics. I have just returned from India where hour after hour the Word of God is preached. Literally hundreds of deaf were hearing, hundreds of cripples were walking, and hundreds of lepers were cleansed.

Even weather conditions changed; one night it rained everywhere except where we walked and drove, and finally when we arrived on the grounds the rain stopped. It was as though a huge lasso of rope had roped off the crusade grounds and would permit no rain to enter. All around the lassoed area it was pouring down rain.

God said, "I'll pour out of my spirit upon all flesh." Then I began to see how some dead churches could sit there and wither away, and while they were withering away, God would be pouring out His Spirit "upon all flesh."

If there is one key word in this outpouring, it is "restoration." The Greek Orthodox Church is on the verge of an spiritual explosion. We are going to see a revival in the Church, and when I say the Church I am not referring to an organization; when I say the Church I am referring to believers gathered from all walks of life, from all faiths and from all denominations, who represent the blood-stained banner of the Cross. Something is going to happen to the Church. You say, "Brother Panos, what is it?" There is coming a great restoration of faith power. That which the lo-

167

cust hath eaten, the cankerworm, and the caterpillar, and the palmer-worm hath eaten and devoured, God is going to restore! "Fear not O land; be glad and rejoice: for the LORD will do great things . . . For he hath given you the former rain moderately, and he will cause to come down for you the former rain, and the latter rain in the first month. And floors shall be full of wheat, and the fats shall overflow with wine and oil. And I will restore to you the years that the locust hath eaten, the cankerworm, and the caterpillar and the palmer-worm" (Joel 2:21-25). God said, "I will restore it. I am going to give it back." When is God going to give it back? In the last days. "In the last days, saith God, "I will pour out of my spirit upon all flesh."

But there is one thing that is very important. Timing! Timing! Don't miss it. If ever there was a time when we needed to get on our face, to get on our hands and our knees before God, in crying, in weeping, in repenting, it is now. Now is the time for us to cry out, "God, let me examine every one of my earthly ambitions!" If there was a time that we were to stand before God and ask God to let our life come into true focus, it is now. If ever there was a time when we must die out to self, it is now! If there ever was a time when we wanted that corn of wheat, our life, to fall to the ground and be crucified with Christ, that it might be resurrected with all the fullness and the beauty and the restoration power of the resurrected Son of the Living God, it is now. It is now! It is now! This is God's time for consecration. God is ready now, people. The most important thing about this whole matter of revival is timing. Don't miss God!

"You have not begun to see anything yet!" But how

many of you want to see it? How many of you want to rededicate your life to God?

Beloved, God has so much more for you in your life! Get involved in what God is doing. Get involved in His mighty vision for souls. Get involved with missionary work. Get involved in world wide evangelistic crusade outreaches. Get involved, and see if God does not open up a reservoir of blessing to flow through your life. You haven't seen anything yet!

CHAPTER 15

EYEWITNESS REPORT OF CRUSADES IN INDIA

By Mrs. Chris Panos

June 10, 1972, found us on a jet plane headed for the land of India. This land is forsaken, desolate, dusty, hot, and primitive.

India is a land full of sorrows, poverty, and sickness. It is a dry land where millions of people worship dead gods. In spite of all of these natural obstacles—in spite of disease, death, and poverty—we went to share the good news that God does care for these precious brown-skinned people.

As I sat in the plane my heart was crying out, "Lord, I do not want to see the sickness, poverty, and sorrow."

How I dreaded landing in Bombay! I felt I couldn't bear to witness the miserable conditions of the people in that city.

My heart cried out, "Lord Jesus, help me!"

He then reminded me of Luke 22:42, where Jesus prayed, "Father, if thou be willing, remove this cup from me: nevertheless not my will, but thine, be done."

Jesus had sat in the place where I was sitting.

This greatly encouraged me as I meditated on the scripture God had spoken to my heart. I drew new strength as I remembered the words of Jesus.

"If any man will come after me, let him deny himself, and take up his cross daily, and follow me" (Luke 9:23).

By this time we had landed in Bombay where we took another plane to Hyderabad. There was a joyful party of precious Indians to meet us in Hyderabad. We talked for a few moments and we then took a taxi to our hotel.

Never had my eyes beheld such suffering. It was a sight that I had never even imagined.

I couldn't believe my eyes.

I was speechless!

I felt as though I had glimpsed the very pit of hell.

As I gazed on the hopeless, helpless people dying without Christ my heart was filled with love and His compassion for them. Then I began to understand a little of the reason why Brother Panos feels so driven to bring the Good News of Jesus and His salvation to India.

Here were people dying slow deaths with no hope of salvation, destined to perish. But oh, what hope and joy arose in my heart as I feasted on His precious promise, "For God so loved the world, that he gave his only begotten Son, that whosoever believeth in him should not perish, but have everlasting life" (John 3:16).

Little did I know that there were before me many

nights that my pillow would be wet with tears all night long.

The question that broke my heart was, "Lord, how can we reach these masses of people with so few laborers?" Then the answer came: "The nationals!"

One dear brother, P. M. Samuel, an apostle of five hundred churches, told my husband, "Brother Panos, you are the only one going to the sinner to preach salvation. Many come to India to preach, but they just visit the churches, or they come and preach and teach at our convention. You are one of the very few in the last twenty-five years that has brought a message of salvation, and who has taken the Gospel to the heathen, the unbelievers."

He added, "Brother Panos, the churches in India need your spirit of zeal and fire. They need this same spirit of fire transmitted to the nationals. You are doing the right thing in raising up the nationals, teaching Indians how to reach other Indians, how to reach sinners. Thank God, He sent you."

We proceeded on our journey through the blasting heat of the desert. Our thoughts drifted back almost two thousand years, as we drove past the oxen and carts that in our country are relics of yesteryear. They suggested surroundings similar to those in the days of Jesus. The crippled were hobbling around with only a stick to support them. The blind were rattling their cups and begging for rupees. The twisted and torn bodies of babies lay crying as mothers pitifully looked at us, begging for a rupee or two. The lepers and many old, helpless crippled people walked with their hands, swishing their bodies between their arms. "My God," was my cry, "is there no hope for these who are destined to per-

172

ish in hell?" Then the answer came: thank God, there is hope. And that hope is in the presentation of the Gospel.

We arrived safely, even though a huge truck ran us off the single lane road into a muddy bank of sand. God was with us and protected us. He brought us on our journey safely.

The First-Night Miracles

The circumstances were against us. But, in spite of everything, over ten thousand raised their hands to Jesus Christ. Hallelujah! The deaf were healed by the dozens. One shouted, "I was deaf since birth!"

Another shouted, "I was deaf for forty years, now I hear!" On and on they went.

Under the preaching of the mighty Word of God, the nights passed very quickly. Every night brought new excitement as God healed all manners of diseases. The crusade increased and increased until there was a sea of people. I have never seen so many people gathered together before. They came and sat on the ground like little children, very much interested.

The powerful presence of God hushed and kept the people silent. He filled the very air with His redeeming love.

Every night I would give instructions, teaching the people how to receive and act on the Word of God.

Then Brother Panos would come to the platform and preach the Gospel. I have never in my life heard the

173

Gospel presented so simply, yet so powerfully, under the anointing of the Holy Spirit.

Brother Panos gave such a vivid description of the shed Blood of Jesus Christ. It was so graphic as Brother Panos presented Christ on the Cross, His death, and His resurrection. You could actually feel the people reaching out and drawing toward Christ with all their hearts. Oh! What a joy arose in my heart as Muslims, Hindus, and Buddhists received Jesus Christ as their only Savior! Praise the Lord!

Behold the Mighty Hand of God

By Sunday the crowds had tripled. Reporters from *The Daccan Chronicle, The Hindu,* and *The Indian Express* newspapers came to interview us. Their question was, "How are these miracles taking place?"

On Sunday night the news reporters had their answer. A great breakthrough came to Caddappa, India. Seven insane women broke through the crowds. They were screaming and hollering and trying to break up the crusade. Brother Panos, with an enormous anointing of peace and power, commanded them to fall down on the ground. Like dead women they fell to the ground.

Brother Panos led all of the vast crowd through the sinner's prayer. Then he commanded these women to rise up and be whole. He told the workers to check the miracles and see if they were perfectly sane.

All seven of these women came to the microphone and testified they were free. They cried with joy! I have never seen so many miracles. One young man was a helpless cripple. His legs and toes were twisted. I saw him walk after his toes were made straight. You could still see the hard, leather-like calouses where he had dragged his toes. Oh! What joy to see the mighty hand of God!

I thought I had seen miracles before, and I had. But not like this, night after night. Tumors, growths, and hernias disappeared. Pastor Philip Abraham and Mr. Souiri, who had come from the last crusade in Kurnool, India (and was still talking about the crusade), were there to testify.

The interpreter, G. Purusholtrom, remarked how they had never seen crazy, devil-possessed, insane people healed instantly by a mass miracle prayer. Thank God for this victory in Caddappa, India! "This is not the work of a man," Brother Panos said night after night, "It is the work of the Holy Spirit." Later a national preached, then another, and miracles were still happening. Praise God! It isn't the work of a man, but the work of the Holy Spirit.

APPENDIX

THE CRUSADE IN KANPUR

Kanpur is India's sixth or seventh largest city, with a population of about one million. It is located between Calcutta and New Delhi. It is an industrial city, away from the usual tourist routes. Kanpur is probably quite typical of Indian cities, with its fair share of cows, pigs, goats, and people intermingled, roaming the streets.

Most of the people are Hindus, with a few Muslins, and fewer Christians. One religious group is notorious. The "Araya Samaji" is a radical Hindu sect. It is bitter and vicious against other religions, especially Christianity. People from the Mayor right on down to the man on the street seem to go pale when Araya Samaji is mentioned. According to the local people, by coming to Kanpur we stumbled on the chief concentration of Araya Samaji power in all of India.

Securing a suitable location for an outdoor crusade

was one of our first jobs. We traveled with one of the pastors by tricycle rickshaw to look over the city. He and most of the Christians recommended the Methodist Church compound. A famous preacher had preached to 5,000 people there some years earlier. I would be quite satisfied to preach to 5,000 people, or even just a few for that matter. But this name Araya Samaji kept popping up. They would ruin our meeting, they would cause a riot, we were told, unless we held the meeting on private Christian property. Only a couple of months earlier, two Christian evangelists in the city were murdered by these fanatical Hindus.

I sensed the fear. Satan had intimidated God's children. These Christians needed an overwhelming victory, not in the safety and shelter of a Christian compound, but right out in the devil's territory. We all needed assurance that Christians have "power over all the power of the enemy," as Christ said.

We rode on the rickshaws past a couple of public parks. One impressed me very much. I shouted to the pastor in the rickshaw ahead of us, "This is the one." He replied, "Impossible," but everyone was willing to help and see what God might do. We visited and witnessed to the mayor and other top city officials. Within two days we had written permission from the authorities to use the park.

Meanwhile I learned something more. Not only does Kanpur have a large concentration of Araya Samaji followers, but the park we chose for the crusade is right at the center of their part of town. In fact the huge cement platform we preached from night after night had been dedicated by the Araya Samaji for their use in religious ceremonies. From a human point of view, we

178

chose the worst place in town. But God was preparing everything for a great victory.

The first night of the crusade between 2,000 and 3,000 people gathered in the park. A large banner above the platform announced in two languages "GOD LOVES YOU." Many believed in Christ through the simple presentation of the Gospel. Others needed more. They needed to see God in action. And we needed to see God confirm His Word with signs following. We needed what Jesus had in His meetings: "The blind see, the lame walk, the lepers are cleansed, the deaf hear, the dead are raised, to the poor the Gospel is preached" (Luke 7:22).

That first night I prayed only for the deaf and dumb to be healed. God seems especially merciful to the deaf so that they might have an opportunity to hear and understand the Gospel. I believed that several would be genuinely healed. But God was doing "exceeding abundantly above all" that I had asked. About forty people came to the platform to testify that they or someone they had brought was miraculously and instantly healed by God's power. Several of the testimonies were exciting and deeply moving.

Two sisters, about five or six years old, were dressed identically and came to the meeting. Both were born deaf and dumb. God healed them simultaneously. Their mother was overjoyed.

A girl of thirteen, born deaf and dumb, astonished the crowd as she clearly and loudly repeated words after me. "Jesus" was one of the first words she spoke.

Night after night God wrought astounding miracles. The hump in a girl's back disappeared. The paralyzed and the lame walked and rejoiced.

179

A father told how his ten-year-old boy had been paralyzed as a result of polio. His arms were twisted and withered. His legs were useless. But now every limb was straight and well. The boy was running around like other children.

Excitement in the city continued to grow. The crowd actually doubled every night. Finally, on the fourth night, a Christian bank accountant estimated the crowd to be at least 15,000.

Hundreds of people prayed each night, confessing sin and inviting Christ to be their Savior and Lord. We held morning convert classes from 8:00 to 9:00. These morning meetings exceeded all expectations. Decision cards were distributed, but repeatedly there weren't enough to go around. Up to 500 or 600 attended the morning classes. The day after our last meeting hundreds had already found one of the churches and were inquiring about further meetings.

Meanwhile, what of the Araya Samaji? A couple of times they tried to instigate a riot, but failed. Some Hindu people cornered one of the ringleaders and threatened to beat him if he caused further trouble! On another night specially printed leaflets attacking our message were distributed, but the crowd remained with us.

Each day I was warned not to attend the meeting, as the Araya Samaji were plotting violence. But God stayed the power of the enemy. Unknown to us, some of the radicals brought guns and knives to the meeting. Various ones later testified that while the Word of God was being preached the men with weapons visibly trembled. Hallelujah!

One of my greatest joys in the crusade was to witness

the transformation in the Christians. Many pastors and young men now believe God will help them preach fearlessly with signs following. Their God is alive! And their beaming faces speak their feelings eloquently.

—A Canadian National

Even a Book Couldn't Tell the Story

Dear Rev. Chris Panos,

Greetings in the name of our Lord and Savior Jesus Christ. We are all doing well here by the grace of God and wish the same for you. In this letter I want to tell you my testimony about the crusades conducted by you in Kurnool (India). It is really a great blessing for us to have healing crusades for the first time in our town.

God has done many miracles in this crusade. Many deaf people were healed and now they are able to hear even the lowest tones. (Doctors can do little for those deaf people in spite of all the modern advancements in surgery.) But God healed them instantaneously.

Many officers who attended these crusades were struck with wonder and they gave testimony about the healings. Another great miracle which I appreciated is that people who had been crippled by polio are walking. Doctors can do nothing for them either. God has done many other miracles on the spot like the healing of swellings, tumors, the dumb, leprous. One woman (aged about 35) had had an issue of blood for the last six years. She had taken all sorts of medicines and had visited many physicians and gynecologists; but nobody could stop her bleeding. But our Lord Jesus Christ stopped her bleeding on the spot. Praise the Lord.

Even a book of 200 pages would not be sufficient to write each miracle separately which happened in this town. I had never seen in my life such miracles, though I had heard about them. Many people in this town are very anxious to see you once again.

We pray in the presence of our Lord that He will send you soon again to this place. Praise the Lord for using his servant Chris Panos in a wonderful way. May God use His servant in a wonderful way to preach the Word of God in each corner of the world.

Yours in HIM,

P. Sunkanna, (Dayanandam)
Final Yr. M.B.B.S.
Kurnool Medical College

Crusade In Kurnool

Our Rev. Chris Panos,

During the crusade, we all had a thrilling time. We never in our life time had seen or heard such wonderful deeds done except in Jesus Christ's time . . . The lame walked on the stage throwing away their sticks . . . The dumb from the first instant pronounced the word JESUS . . . and the blind opened their eyes . . . PRAISE BE TO GOD.

We experienced a wonderful time and when you left us on the last day at the grounds, myself and Mr. Souri stood still, watching you go by. You impressed thousands of people of different castes and creeds.

Yes, the multitude *lifted up their voices to Jesus Christ* and *held them up in praise!!!!* When you said with such confidence that the Holy Spirit is by the side of every man and woman, every boy and girl, the presence of the Holy Spirit became very real and *we actually felt Him dwelling in the midst of the multitude.* Jesus lived among us.

I used to feel gloomy, but during those ten precious days, I had a new experience. Now I have no fears or anxieties, just *joy* and *peace!*

Whenever we met other people, we recalled what you said after each event and miracle: "Who did this? Who accomplished this miracle?" The whole crowd, including those healed, shouted in joy and awe ... JESUS ... JESUS ... JESUS ... JESUS. The name of JESUS CHRIST resounded in praise thousands and thousands and thousands of times every day. It was a sight to see all the Hindus, Muslims, Communists and Christians *raising their hands* in unison and accepting JESUS, asking Him to come into their hearts.

On the outset of your crusade meeting, you introduced our Lord in a different way. It was so majestic to say, "From the very first night, I want you to know I am not a politician. I have not come 15,000 miles to talk to you about politics, but I have come to talk to you about the King of Kings and Lord of Lords. His name is JESUS."

I liked the way you began. Your picture of God's love and JESUS on the Cross was so graphic, proclaiming, "By His stripes we are healed"; We, too, had read the door was closed to white missionaries, but now we know the door is closed to the old, obsolete ways of preaching the Gospel. You brought before us the only way the Gospel can be successfully preached in mass media.

You so vividly made it clear that, "IT IS NOT THE WORK OF CHRIS PANOS ... BUT THE WORK OF THE BLESSED HOLY SPIRIT," and when you extended your crusade and announced that Rev. Purusholtrom would continue, not many believed that he would be able to produce the same results. But thank God, it all came to pass. Oh thank God, the last night the Crusade closed with 50,000 people standing in the rain four hours. Truly this is not the work of any man. It is the sovereign work of the Holy Spirit.

God bless you, your wife and children for the magnificent service done in His name.

Mrs. Beula Souri

"Inspired and Challenged"

My Beloved Brothers and Sisters in Christ and Chris Panos,

In Kurnool, India, we held a mass crusade in the month of April. God's servant, Chris Panos, preached the Living Word. Truly this God-given ministry was deeply appreciated by all. In all my thirty years of ministry I never saw so many outstanding miracles. This was the first mass crusade in Kurnool. The people of Kurnool were taken by surprise. Never before had the people seen such great miracles as hundreds of deaf and

184

dumb were healed. Blind eyes were opened, cripples instantly walked, and leprous people were cleansed. I can say truly that this was an earth-shaking experience for the people of India, as Muslims, Hindus, Christians, and Communists all sat together in peace crying out to Jesus Christ to come into their hearts. By the third night a multitude of 40,000 people were attending. The crusade inspired and challenged many Chrisitan ministers and gave them a new outlook toward the Gospel.

Then Brother Panos announced that the national brother G. Purusholtrom, would preach the next four nights. The miracles continued to happen. This truly proved to all the truth that Brother Panos was stressing, "This is not the work of a man, but this is the work of the Holy Spirit."

Now it was coming to pass and one of my co-workers, though he had interpreted before and held minor crusades by laying on of hands, was now preaching the Gospel to the masses successfully. The last night proved that Brother Panos was led of God to challenge us to launch out to win souls in great effectiveness.

Your Friend and Brother in Christ,

Pastor Philip Abraham*

The Miracles Continue

My dear brothers and sisters in Christ,

God is alive with great power. My testimony is so simple. My whole desire has always been to win souls and

* Pastor Abraham is an overseer of many churches—ED.

see all the churches full. I want to tell you how it came to pass that I was preaching to 50,000 people who stood four hours in the rain on the last night. To tell the truth, I was afraid to try to continue the crusade in response to Brother Panos's word. I did not really know what to do in a mass crusade. But our miraculous God enabled me to go forward. Then I perfectly understood that "this is the Lord's doing." All the people, including myself, thought the miracles would stop and the people wouldn't come after Brother Panos left. But "this is the Lord's doing," and it was really marvelous to my eyes as I witnessed people being healed by the Lord through the impartation of God's Word through His servant's preaching.

Now I have a new faith and vision to conduct such crusades throughout the land of India and among all the Gentiles. The first night I preached, we witnessed a huge gathering of about 30,000. After learning for sure how to preach the Gospel, I preached to the whole crowd and taught them the "sinner's prayer." Then I offered prayer for the deaf and inquired of them if there was healing. Thirty people raised their hands to show that they were healed. Some of them had been deaf from birth. In the same manner the blind received sight and the lame began to leap. One man rushed to the rostrum from his house which was located at a distance. Excitedly he said, "I heard an announcement from the speaker to lay hands on any growth. I too had a big growth over my neck. I laid my hands on my neck in the bathroom while the prayer was being prayed. To my astonishment I felt the growth melt away like ice in my hand as the growth went down and down."

Praise the Lord, brothers and sisters. You, too, can have this kind of miracle ministry.

G. Purusholtrom*

From a Medical Student

Dear Rev. Chris Panos,

Greetings in the name of our Lord Jesus Christ Who is our savior. I am happy here and wish the same with you.

By the grace of our Living God we had healing at Kurnool Town. Thousands of people gathered for these meetings. God used you wonderfully. This is the first time that I have seen such a great healing crusade. God has given me a little opportunity to work in the meetings. Thanks to our Lord. These healing crusades were from April 7 to April 16.

I saw many miracles, like deaf hearing, cripples walking, dumb people talking, blind people seeing. And especially one, a woman who had had an issue of blood for six years, was healed on the spot.

Not only the above miracles but also thousands of Hindu, Muslim, and different kinds of people who hate Christianity praised our Living God on seeing all the miracles that have taken place during your healing crusade. Even today many people were asking me about your next campaign for Kurnool. Please let me know about your next campaign for India.

* Brother Purusholtrom is the national who learned that he too could preach to large crowds, with the same results as Chris Panos—ED.

We wish you all a great success in your next crusade in the near future. Kindly pray for me.

Yours in Him,

T. G. Paul (M.B.S.S.)
Kurnool Medical College.

Suggested Inspirational
Paperback Books

THE ACTS OF THE GREEN APPLES
by Jean Stone Willans $1.45
Once upon a time, the Willanses were quiet, respectable suburbanites. The story of how they got to Hong Kong is the heartwarming miracle-studded and frankly hilarious account of *The Acts of the Green Apples*.

CLIMB MOUNT MORIAH
by Pat Brooks $1.25
A fascinating study of people who have passed through life's darkest moments, facing prospects of broken marriage and adultery, financial ruin and disgrace. They learned how to tap vast reservoirs of spiritual power and come through to victory—and so can you!

FACE UP WITH A MIRACLE
by Don Basham $1.25
This is a fascinating book about God the Holy Spirit bringing a new dimension into the lives of twentieth-century Christians. It is filled with experiences that testify to a God of miracles being unleashed in our lives right now.

GILLIES' GUIDE TO HOME PRAYER MEETINGS
by George and Harriet Gillies $1.25
He is a retired Wall Street executive. She is his wife. Together, they wrote *A Scriptural Outline of the Baptism in the Holy Spirit*. Now the Gillies bring us this practical, step-by-step handbook dealing with the problems and procedures involved in setting up the kind of home fellowship that will bless the lives of all attending.

HOW GREAT I WAS!
by Doug Foley $1.25
Doug Foley was a young, ambitious engineer who woke up one morning to find all his dreams shattered by the words of a neurologist who told him, "You've got disseminated sclerosis." *How Great I Was* is the gripping true story of the miracles that brought Doug Foley back to health in spirit, mind, and body.

HE SPOKE AND I WAS STRENGTHENED
by Dick Mills $1.25
An easy-to-read devotional of 52 prophetic scripturally-based messages directed to the businessman, the perfectionist, the bereaved, the lonely, the ambitious and many more.

IF I CAN, YOU CAN
by Betty Lee Esses $2.25
The wife of charismatic teacher Michael Esses tells how Jesus saved her husband and her marriage and shares what He's been teaching the Esses ever since. For Betty, these were hard-won spiritual insights. For you, they can come easy; all you have to do is read this book.

IF YOU SEE LENNIE
by Char Potterbaum $1.45
Char Potterbaum was so full of pills her husband claimed she rattled when she turned over in bed. Learn why she doesn't need pills anymore—and how she exchanged her depression for joy—in a book that combines everyday, homespun humor with true spiritual wisdom.

KICKED OUT OF THE KINGDOM
by Charles Trombley $1.25
It all began with a totally unexpected *miracle*—healing of his baby daughter's clubbed feet. Trombley's Jehovah's Witness friends said, "The devil did it!" But Trombley asked, "Would the devil do anything as beautiful as this?" From beginning to end, this is the story of God's sovereign move in the life of a man who really wanted to know the truth.

LET GO!
by Fenelon 95¢
Jesus promised a life full of joy and peace. Why then are so many Christians struggling to attain the qualities that Christ said belonged to the child of God? Fenelon speaks firmly—but lovingly—to those whose lives have been an uphill battle. Don't miss this one.

A MANUAL ON EXORCISM
by H. A. Maxwell Whyte $1.25
The Exorcist posed the question; this book has the answers. Are there really such things as demons? How can you know if you have one? Can anybody cast out demons? These and many more troublesome questions are clearly answered in this helpful book.

THE NEW WINE IS BETTER
by Robert Thom $1.45
Anyone with problems (and who hasn't got problems?) needs to read this story of one man who saw the invisible, believed the incredible, and received the impossible. A lively and often amusing account of Robert Thom's downward trek from a 12 bedroom mansion in South Africa to the hopeless world of an alcoholic on the verge of suicide—and the whole new world of faith and power Robert Thom discovered after Mrs. Webster came knocking on his door.

PLEASE MAKE ME CRY
by Cookie Rodriguez $1.45
The first female dope addict to "kick the habit" in Dave Wilkerson's ministry, Cookie was so hard people said even death didn't want her. Told the way it really happened, this is the true story of how Cookie found Someone she wanted even more than heroin.

THE PURPLE PIG AND OTHER MIRACLES
by Dick Eastman $1.45
Hidden away in a rambling, wood-frame house on "O" Street in Sacramento, there is a special underground room where Bible-believing Christians pray twenty-four hours a day, seven days a week. Miracles? They happen all the time. And the prayer power is spreading . . .

THE RAPTURE BOOK
by Doug Chatham $1.25
Almost everybody seems agreed that old planet Earth is a time-bomb about to go off, but here's a different slant—a slant which is backed up by the age-old prophecies of the Bible. Exciting teaching about the next event on the prophetic calendar!

SCANDALOUS SAINT
by John C. Hagee $1.25
It all started at the tender age of 4, when John Eils got his picture in the newspapers a notoriously young "culprit." From that time on, he was into one hair-raising scrape after another. Arrested for using a sound truck, jailed for smuggling contraband into Mexico, charged with using his church as a house of prostitution his story proves that a saint's life isn't necessarily dull!

SEVEN SPLENDID MOMENTS
by Carmen Benson $1.25
Plain days and dragging hours can come alive with beauty and splendor—if you know the secret. We think you'll find the secret in this book, a collection of intimate and true short stories designed to acquaint you with God's perfect Truth.

SIMMER DOWN, SAINT
by Jody Woerner $1.25

Anxious? Uptight? Lost your cool? Simmer down—and learn how to add health, strength, peace and joy to your everyday living as the author shares with you a series of insights designed to steer you away from the wrong turns and potholes scattered along the straight and narrow way.

THE SPIRIT-LED FAMILY
by Grace Robley and Wendell (Rob) Robley, M.D. $1.25

Family life doesn't have to be a contest, pitting one member's interests against another's. If your family life isn't all you want it to be, this book will show you how you, too, can experience the love, peace, joy which is meant to be yours.

----WHEREVER PAPERBACKS ARE SOLD OR USE THIS COUPON-----

Whitaker House

504 LAUREL DRIVE, MONROEVILLE, PA 15146

SEND INSPIRATIONAL BOOKS LISTED BELOW

Title   Price   ☐ Send Complete Catalog

_____   _____

_____   _____

_____   _____

_____   _____

_____   _____

_____   _____

_____   _____

NAME_____

STREET_____

CITY_____STATE_____ZIP_____